A Road So Travelled

Brian G. Davies

PURPLE UNICORN MEDIA

Published by Purple Unicorn Media

Copyright © 2022 by Brian G. Davies

All rights are reserved.
No part of this publication may be reproduced, stored in a retrieval system or transmitted in any form or by any means, electronic, mechanical, photocopying, recording or otherwise, without prior permission of the publisher.

ISBN 978-1-910718-19-3

Cover image: The Nexxo by a French lake enroute to Italy

To Family, Past, Present & Future

Where-ever they may be

Table of Contents

Preface

Section A: Personal and Family

Times Remembered – Early Lives
Memories of a Wartime Childhood
Memories of Kings School, Ely in the Wartime 1940s
Looking Back – National Service and Me
Brian – The Autobiography
Doris Mabel Davies – A Biography
Doris Mabel Davies – Notes About Her Life
Colin's Life Story – Part 1: 1939 to 1945
Colin's Life Story – Part 2: From August 1952
Stories by Imogen Dudley (age 9)
Poems by Bethan K (then a Teenager)
Christmas
Coming Home – A Hymn

Section B: Travel

Land of the Breton
The Welsh Borders – The Marches
The Pilgrim Route to Compostela
Singapore: The Lion City
Dream On In Canada
East Germany (2 articles)
Exploring The Massif Central
To Florence and Pisa in a Nexxo
A Yorkshire Odyssey
A Quick Look at Lancaster
Mediterranean Cruising (2 articles)
Seeking the Northern Lights
Second Helpings of Turkey
A Glimpse of Heaven
Italy – Top to Toe
Our Scottish Holiday

Cruising The Mekong River
A Visit to Carew Castle and Tenby
Llandudno
Cruising Around the Bay of Biscay

Section C: Interest

Our Life in Motorhomes
Hidden Treasure – Hales View Farm
Development of the Westgate Chronicle
Sawney Bean, a Scottish Cannibal
The Mumbles Railway

About the Author

Preface

For over two years, my father Brian G. Davies worked with me on putting this book together. The three-section format was to enable family history to be featured in the first part, and miscellaneous articles to be the focus of the third. The bulk of the book was the middle section, the many holidays he and my mother, and after her death, mostly he and my sister's family had been on. These articles include ones published in other magazines at the time, but for many of these we were working from PDFs or JPGs and had to retype the whole text. Photographs had to be matched up to the articles, and in many cases needed to be scanned in, or found from archives. It was truly my father's Magnum Opus and he often said that he hoped that it would not be posthumous. I was able to get a printed proof into his hands as he lay in hospital, but tragically he died a few weeks before the final edition was ready to go to print. He knew that it soon would be, and his spirit presents this book to you all.

With all my love as his Editor

Jon Davies

Times Remembered – Early Lives

On the evening of 30th November 1936, the Crystal Palace burnt to the ground. I remember being held up by my father, and sitting on his shoulders, to watch the glow in the sky. At the time our home was a 3-bedroomed terraced house in Charlecote Grove, a small cul-de-sac off Kirkdale in Sydenham, South London.

Charlecote Grove

My infant education was at nearby Kelvin Grove Junior School and, although only 5 at the time, was able to walk alone to school and back quite safely, despite having to cross Kirkdale, quite a major road but not too busy in those days. My father was a police constable stationed not too far away in Lower Kirkdale, on the way to Forest Hill, and my mother was a teacher. She had to travel by No.49 bus to Tooting Bec, and then take a tube train to Colliers Wood, where she was deputy head. It was a long journey and, as she would arrive home after me, I was usually looked after by Mrs. Groves, who lived in one of the older terraced houses across the road. Because of the problems this arrangement caused, my younger brother Colin had for some while been living with our paternal grandparents in Neath, South Wales, where I would join him for the summer holidays.

Air Raid Shelter in Charlecote Grove

The years between 1936 and 1939 were filled with rumours of war with Germany. Towards the end there was much evidence of this in the numerous sandbags becoming available, railings being cut down and collected for the "war effort", and windows in private homes and on public transport being protected by strips of sticky tape or by a close-woven adhesive net. On 3rd September 1939 the Prime Minister, Neville Chamberlain, came on the wireless to announce that "We are at war!" My parents thought that I too would be safer (and no doubt less trouble) living in Neath also, and for the rest of that school year I lived at Creswell Road, Neath, attending with Colin the Gnoll Junior School. Life with my grandparents was quite basic – gas lamp lighting downstairs and none upstairs. We had to carry our candlesticks to bed…we slept together in the large front bedroom as Uncle Will, actually a cousin of my father's, occupied the other spare bedroom. The only toilet was outside down the yard, with old newspapers earning their keep, so we had a 'guzzunder' – a po – kept under the bed for nighttime emergencies. Washing was carried out by way of a jug and ewer, with warm water being brought up to us by "Gramma", as she was known to us, or a rinse under the cold water outside tap. "Dada" was a railwayman, and spent his spare time sitting by the fire in the scullery, smoking his pipe.

My Grandparents, John and Sarah Davies

It was in here too that we ate, as the middle room was shared between Uncle Will, who would both eat his meals there and bathe in the evenings. and Gramma, who was a home-based seamstress. Upstairs was her workroom, known as "The Office"….actually a leftover from the days when my father ran his coal merchant business from home. The front room was sacrosanct, therefore out of bounds to us and only in use on special occasions.

Dada had a dog, a large brown Alsatian called Jack, who had been trained to take the shopping basket in his teeth and trot down the road to the grocer's shop on the corner. There the grocer would take the money, read the shopping list and put the required items into Jack's basket, whereupon he would proudly return home with it. Uncle Will kept an aviary in the back garden and I often helped him feed the canaries and budgies with boiled egg yolk mixed with seed. Colin and I often played in the street with other children; particular friends were a boy called Leighton and a girl called Rita, who lived next door to the grocer. I remember tying a cord to our knocker, and then to the one across the street, and then pulling the cord. I was not popular with the adults for a while after that. One day at school Colin was seized with bad stomach cramps and I, not to be outdone, got them also, so we were both sent home. Here it transpired that Colin had appendicitis whilst I had only come out 'in sympathy'. From then on I think my behaviour became worse; I remember on one occasion fighting with Gramma on the stairs, refusing to do what I was told. I presume that Gramma told my parents that she could no longer control both of us and carrying on working so I was taken back home, only then to join the horde of evacuees in September 1940 who were being sent out of London to presumably safer destinations. I recall standing, with many other children, on Paddington station platform, a label attached to me, and a gasmask box looped around my neck. My parents must have been with me, but I don't recall any fond (or other) farewells.

Uncle Will with Colin and Brian

I do however recall arriving, co-incidentally, at Neath station again. Uncle Will, who was well up with local grapevine, met the train, and no doubt comforted me as I, with many others, was led to a bus. We were ferried up the Neath valley to the small mining village of Cwmgrach, and debussed into the Junior School there, to await our turn at being chosen as a villager's evacuee. So began the next chapter of my young life, as it turned out a not very happy one. My 'uncle' was a miner, and 'auntie' was very strong on 'Chapel', often leaving me on Sunday evenings to fend for myself – outside! I was fortunate, however, that some weekends Uncle Will would come up by bus to take me back to Creswell Road, where my brother Colin was still living; without such trips life as an evacuee would have been rather miserable, and he and I would have become even more estranged. However, on one occasion my parents came to see how things were. I remember we all climbed the incline to the colliery coal tip behind Cwmgrach to look back over the village. I think that visit might have had some bearing on my next relocation, for in September 1941 I was sent off to boarding school at Ely, near Cambridge.

At Cwmgrach

Memories of a Wartime Childhood

I was almost six years old at the start of the Second World War. In 1930 my parents had moved from South Wales to London, for my father to join the Metropolitan Police. My earliest memory was of November 1936, and my father holding me up to see, in the night sky, the glow of Crystal Palace burning – a portent of the coming war years? In 1939, like many others living in the London area, my parents sent my brother and I out of the capital to our grandparents back in Wales. They, however, were too old to look after both of us so, after several months, I was returned to London, to await my next transportation.

In 1940, and just before my seventh birthday, I was taken to Paddington Station, to join many hundreds of other children, most with labels attached. This was the start of the great evacuation, and soon I was being transported, this time at the authorities' discretion, back to South Wales. When the train stopped at Neath I was met by my Uncle Will, but then we were bussed fifteen miles or so up the valley to a small Welsh mining village, where we congregated in the school hall. Here, the villagers had the pick of us, and I ended up with a strict chapel-going middle-aged couple, with a grown-up daughter also living at home. It was not the ideal situation for a young boy and, with my brother still living with my grandparents not so far away in Neath, I spent quite a bit of time bussing between the two locations.

Eventually, of course, the situation deteriorated, and in 1941 I was withdrawn and sent to a boarding-school in East Anglia. Here I spent the next four years, going back to my home in London at holiday time. Thankfully I had missed The Blitz, but I still have memories of being bombed by incendiaries, landmines, doodle-bugs (V1's) and even a V2, which landed one Saturday afternoon in an adjacent street, obliterating a block of flats and the children's party within. Much time was spent in the shelters, either the Anderson in next-door's garden, the block at the end of the street, or our own Morrison shelter in our bedroom. My mother was a teacher, and part of my summer holiday was spent at her school, for my own had longer holidays. One day our bus was machine-gunned by a low-flying German fighter (luckily it missed us!); another day we returned home to find the houses opposite in ruins from the blast of another V2 which had landed in the school fields behind them. Unfortunately, this was a common sight around.

At home, my father had the ubiquitous chicken shed in the back garden, with Rhode Island Reds and Leghorns providing much-needed eggs. He also had an allotment at the end of the street, where my brother and I loved to play when we were reunited during summer holidays. Back at boarding-school, however, food was adequate and nutritious, and my meagre pocket-money even stretched to sticky buns and packets of Symington's Soup from the tuck shop. War was often not too far away, however, with the occasional V1 doodling across the night sky, the remains of a crashed German bomber by the river's edge, and at the start of Michaelmas Term 1944 one of my friends failed to return from his holiday….in London. Germany surrendered in May 1945 and, possibly in an effort to bring about another surrender, I joined with several friends in "drowning" the Japanese flag in a nearby water tank (we had to wait until August for that one!).

I moved back home in the summer of 1945 in time to join my new school in South London, and indeed to move house too, and for my brother to rejoin the family. There was much to be thankful for, as we had all come through relatively unscathed, if not unscarred. None of my relations had been enlisted in the Services, and I was the first to join the Armed Forces, in 1952, but that, as they say, is another story.

Memories of Kings School, Ely in the Wartime 1940s

PROLOGUE

During the early months of 1939, rumours of war with Germany had been rife. That country had been re-arming itself for some years, and now was about to expand its borders by suborning its neighbours. The Sudetenland had gone, as had both Austria and the rest of Czechoslovakia and Poland was next on Herr Hitler's list. Our Prime Minister, Neville Chamberlain, had returned from his conference in Munich waving a piece of paper bearing Hitler's promise not to invade Poland, but at the end of August it became clear to all that this was not to hold. Britain had committed itself to the defence of Poland, should it become necessary, so, on 3rd September 1939, just after Germany had invaded that country, Britain pre-empted matters by declaring war on Germany.

My parents were both working people, with good jobs, and were reluctant to take any time off from those while having to take care of two small children, so my 3-yr. old brother and myself, then 5, were sent down to South Wales to live, temporarily at least, with our father's parents. Also in the household was 'Uncle' Will, who had been brought up with my father, but the 4-bedroom house in Neath was large enough to accommodate us all, in safety, if not in complete comfort. There was no indoor plumbing, the toilet was a lean-to in the back garden, and the only lighting was from gas mantles downstairs. Still, it was away from the bombing in London, and only for a short time anyway……

Sad to say, I did not settle comfortably, and after a period now known as the "Phony War", I was sent back to my parents in London, Gramma saying she could no longer control me. Colin, still only 4, was a different proposition, and remained with our grandparents for the whole of the war. But my parents still had to get me sorted, and took advantage of the Government's plan to evacuate mothers and children to safer places away from London. In September 1940 I found myself at Paddington railway station, with my parents bidding me a relieved if not very fond farewell and, complete with gasmask in its cardboard box around my neck, I set off on another phase in my somewhat disturbed life. Strangely co-incidentally I, together with many other children, were de-trained at Neath railway station, to be put on buses for the next stage, this time to Cwmgrach, a small mining village in the Swansea valley. Here we were unloaded into the village school, where prospective 'uncles' and 'aunties' looked us over, selecting which of us they would like to take home. Eventually I was put into the hands of one lady and walked to her home not too far away, where I was to remain until the next hiccup in my formative life.

****

In the summer of 1941 my parents took me from that small South Wales village, where the authorities had sent me from London, and where I had spent a not very happy year, and passed me at the age of eight into the not-so-tender care of Mr. Cross, headmaster of the King's School, Ely, Cambs at the time. He was a Latin specialist (had in fact written the school text-book on the subject) and I was not, so our out-of-lesson meetings tended to be quite painful, for me anyway. He was quite handy with the slipper!!

Entrance to the School

My first memory at the school, having struggled up Back Hill from the railway station, was a staged fight with a boy called Belcher. He was Jewish, and I was Welsh, so it became something of a racial issue, for the spectators anyway. Neither of us knew any of them, and couldn't care less, so one punch and it was over. Belcher sat and I was cheered, then both of us 'new bugs' were on our own. There were four houses then…..Burns, Boultbee (where I was put), Ingle and Ivatt. By the time I joined the school Eton College-type dress had been done away with, and for us it was grey flannel shorts and jackets. Soon I was to meet Matron, her assistant Minnie, and my mentor Stutter. He and his friend Hyde took me under their wing and taught me to do the 'Dead Man's Dive' from the top board of the now-defunct open-air swimming pool located somewhere near to the station.

Brian aged 8, at Ely

That was before I learned to swim, which Stutter then got me doing quite soon afterwards. I also learned to ride a bicycle; it belonged to Gamon (funny, but first names hardly ever registered, and were rarely used). A few practice sessions on the school playing field saw me up and running. I don't think it was long, however, before disaster struck. I used to get up early on Sunday mornings, borrow the bike and cycle down to the river. On re-entering the school one morning I forgot the brakes were dicey, and ran the bike down the drive and straight into the wall outside the Headmaster's House….didn't do its front wheel any good at all.

Cathedral and School (in later times)

one of those combined desks). Below us was the Middle Porta, where some lessons were more intimately held. It was however at times a good change to go over to the more modern Hill House, with its light and airy classroom, and in which I remember Geography and English classes being held. For science there was the trip across the road to Hereward House (now Old Hereward), adjacent to which in Silver Street was the tuck shop. Sticky buns and Symington's soup were for some reason high on my shopping list there. Top Porta was also used for the school plays, and I do recall watching one - "The Monkey's Paw" – there one evening. But, apart from the weekly crocodile to the Cathedral. The only times I got into Ely town itself were, once on an official trip to see a performance of "The Mikado", and once to take tea in the Lamb Hotel on a rare occasion of my parents' visit. I do believe though that other boys were at times more adventurous than I. Punishment for breaking bounds could be severe, and of that slipper I had experienced my fill.

In those days the dining hall was in a kind of undercroft, where the Memorial Library is now. Evenings of buns and cocoa before going to bed in the dormitory above (the Cubicles, though they had by then been removed). One memory is of the fire smouldering at one end of the dorm, with boys making shadowy animals on the wall. And listening to jokes, and ghost stories, before Minnie checked that we had completed our toilet and settled us down for the night. I also recall that, at least once a year, we had to be weighed; this involved waiting in our pyjamas in the dorm, before being called to a room opposite, where Mr. Cross and matron had set up scales. To access this we had to divest ourselves and cling, naked, to a hook whilst being suspended until our weight registered, then – pyjamas back on– back to the dorm.

Form photograph with Mr Smith

Mr. Smith was our Form Master, and amongst boys of my age were Gamon (of the bike), little Groom, JWVCoston, Waddington, Hipwell and Peter Morton. Other names I recall were Heritage, Calnan, Taylor, Ross, Everitt, Lambourne and the 'day bug' Dawson, some of which can be spotted on the attached photo – no prizes for spotting ME…the gormless-looking one! All are now shadowy memories of 'happier' days, and how many are still with us, I wonder? More senior names are Boorman (there were two of them), Angwin (was he Head Boy then?), Lacy, Goodin, Bridges and Huggins. A few of them I can still bring to mind, perhaps because of their involvement with the school's rowing team on the river Ouse.

At some stage I changed dormitories, moving to the top floor of the Priory, and overlooking the Priory garden, at the far end of which was an old yew tree in which I spent quite a few weekend hours clambering amongst its sturdy branches. I do have a photo of me, complete with bow and arrow, standing on the lawn here taken, I presume, on one of the occasions when my parents came to visit. The dormitory window gave access onto the roof of the bay below and I remember being an observer (honest!) whilst one of our less popular dorm-mates, in a state of complete undress and, having had black boot-polished applied to his more private parts, was forcibly ejected onto it. Bath time over here was on the ground floor, with old-fashioned hip baths, and sliding about on our naked bottoms when tipping out the soapy water across the smooth floor was great fun.

Brian on his 9th birthday, 1942

My only remembrances of the war whilst at Kings were, one night when lying awake in our top-floor dormitory, we heard a lonely and no doubt lost bomber make its way above the Cathedral, and shed its load somewhere onto an adjacent field before making for its home in Germany. And one other night when we heard the phut-phut of a passing doodle-bug, before it cut out and dropped harmlessly many miles away. Also in my memory is that of a bonfire on the Triangle outside the Porta at the war' end, and drowning the Japanese flag in one of the huge NFS water-tanks there. Otherwise, the war was, in our little cocoon, too far away to worry us.

Some teachers still stick in one's memory. Like Miss Arber, who took us for Geography, Mr. Osmond, for Science over in Hereward House, and where we saw some spectacular experiments (collapsing tins and such like). Mrs Osmond who, I believe, read Dr. Doolittle to us, and the Rev. Burgess who in the Priory taught me to play the piano. Regrettably I do not recall the name of the Maths master who lived across the road from the school (near to day-bug Dawson who, on occasion, invited me to his house to play with a construction kit…no, not Lego, the other one!.) Nor the mistress who took us for English (poetry and Spelling B's) in Hill House, though strangely I DO remember sections of poetry we learned with her. I also remember Mr. Wilkinson (Wilkie – he kindly accommodated me for a night several years later whilst I was on a cycle tour around Middle England prior to my being called up for National Service), who taught Games and English and, of course, the aforesaid Mr. Cross, who was also our Scoutmaster. My two memories here are of re-raffiating chair seats in a very small room somewhere at the top of Headmasters' House, and of going to scout camp in the Lake District one summer holiday, bathing naked in a freezing cold stream, making porridge in a Dixie, and endless treks. Then home through the wartime blackout, changing trains at Crewe, and sleeping on the carriage floor in almost pitch darkness whilst the train made its stuttering way back to London. Living there, I spent almost all my holidays with the aerial war on my doorstep. We were almost bombed out twice by V.1 s (the doodlebugs), almost eliminated by a V2….. remember them? A flash of light, and the world stood still before erupting in a crescendo of frenzy and fury. The street next to ours vanished one peaceful Sunday afternoon. I wondered at times which of my schoolmates would not be returning next term…..never myself, though.

I have not kept in touch with any of my school contemporaries, although I did once try to trace Peter Morton at Thetford (if he was the right one). So it must say something about my attachment to King's that, despite only attending for my Junior school years, I still remember my days there quite clearly…even now, at my advanced octogenarian age. When living in Peterborough some years ago my late wife and I did visit King's on an Open Day, and were treated to excellent hospitality. I do keep an eye open for email, but unfortunately, now living at a distance from Ely, it is unlikely that I shall be able to visit again. Still, memory (whilst I still have it) can be a wonderful thing!

National Service and Me

Back in the early Fifties I received my call-up papers for National Service, and travelled to the Tower of London where I was to spend my early days in the Army. I had been posted to the Royal Fusiliers (City of London Regiment), which was based here, and where I began my Basic Training. This appeared to consist of polishing the wooden floor of our accommodation, learning how to blanco our webbing and polish our brasses, polish our boots until we could see our faces in them, and how to make our beds to the required standard. In between these activities we had rifle drill on the parade ground and weapons training in the surrounding (dry) moat, both open to scrutiny by the general public.

Following this rather rudimentary introduction to the start of my two-year break from civilian life, I was posted to the Royal East Kent Regiment, (known as The Buffs). Here I learned how to march, how to strip down a Bren gun – and reassemble it, how to fire a Sten gun, how to set a minefield, to become familiar with the intricacies of our friend the '303 rifle, and the basics of armed and unarmed combat. I was even selected for officer training (OCTU) but decided that at least on the grounds of cost alone it was not for me, and opted instead for acceptance at the Beaconsfield depot of the Royal Army Education Corps. At the end of my training here I was to be posted as a Sergeant to Germany, but at the last minute it was discovered that I had not gained a pass in Mathematics in the School Certificate exams before leaving school. This lapse in my educational achievements resulted in a delay while I sat the

Army's 1st Class Certificate in that subject. Being successful at this I was now eligible for the **next** draft, which was to the Far East, and soon I found myself on the troopship Empire Pride.

Brian in Singapore

I was initially sent to REME lines, where I had my first encounter with the Sergeants' Mess and my first sleep under a mosquito net. It was here too that my next posting was under review – Singapore city, up-country Malaya, or Hong Kong. Eventually it was Singapore, and I was directed to the barracks of the Army Guard Dog Unit, somewhat out in the wilds. Nominally it came under the aegis of the RAVC, with a vet constantly on duty. However, the main purpose of the soldiers' duties was to provide armed guards to the various military installations in and around the island which could be attacked by insurgents In this they were supported by a variety of fierce-looking dogs, which by day were kept locked in their pens unless required for other activities – exercise, demonstrations or medical appointments.

My primary work included preparing the men for possible promotion (by way of the Army's 3rd Class certificate) and education ranged through English and Mathematics and map-reading to general subjects such as an appreciation of the political situation in Malaysia. But I also had responsibility for the further education of senior ranks at a near-by RAMC (medical) depot, to where I had to travel by land-rover with my Malay driver. In barracks I had an office, my own room, and was more-or-less my own master. Outside work hours I was free to visit and enjoy the sights of the city itself. I joined in Army life, representing the Unit at darts, playing cricket, and refereeing inter-unit football matches, as well as becoming the unit's unofficial photographer – many of the men wanted photos of themselves with their dogs to send back home.

The Empire Fowey

Life continued to smile on me, and twenty-one months later, after declining an offer to extend my tour by another year, I was homeward bound on a much better class of troopship, the Empire Fowey. It was back to Beaconsfield, and demob time. Two years for which I would be always grateful, as it taught me independence, and had given me a taste for overseas travel which I never really lost. I had joined up straight from school as a callow youth……now I was an experienced adult who had exercised responsibility for the educational welfare of men in an overseas posting.

<u>Brian G. Davies - ex RAEC Sgt/Instructor</u>

Brian – The Autobiography

Back in the summer of 1952, I was coming to the end of my Secondary schooling. In September 1941, at the age of almost twelve, I had transferred from the King's School, Ely to Alleyn's Grammar School and had spent the subsequent years following a not very successful academic career. In those days, G.C.E.'s were important; at my first attempt I actually acquired four passes. But certificates were then only given for five passes, so the following year I had to re-sit. Fortunately, rules had been changed, and although I still only achieved four passes, I was able in the following term to re-sit – and pass – a further two subjects, bringing the total to six. Still not a wonderful achievement, but it did at least permit me to enter the sixth form, albeit a year late. Here, in my first year, I sat two A-level subjects, but obtained a pass in only one (English L). As a result, it was decided, either by my Headmaster or by my parents (or possibly both), that I had reached the pinnacle of my academic achievement, and that, when the call came to begin my National Service, I would respond to it.

After my attempt at the two A-level subjects had ended, there were still a couple of weeks to the end of term, so I decided to take some time off and do a bit of cycling. First I cycled to Ely, where I stayed a couple of nights with 'Wilky' Wilkinson, my erstwhile English teacher. My next target was more ambitious, and as I cycled through the fens I wondered if I had not aimed a bit too high. However, I made it to the outskirts of Leicester, where I stayed with a friend whom I had met a couple of years earlier at a Crusader House Party. Then came the hard part, crossing the Pennines, At the start of the hilly section I did what we all tried in those days…hanging onto the back of the lorry, and trusting that I would not be spotted. But spotted I was by the driver himself who, fortunately, became sympathetic when I explained my destination and, loading my bike into the back of his vehicle, gave me a lift to the outskirts of Liverpool. From here it was only a short trip to the New Brighton home of a boy who had been in my tent the previous year, and with whom I stayed for the next couple of days.

It was while here that I was stopped on the estate by a policeman for NOT halting at a 'STOP' sign. I was given an official warning, and in return I gave him a false address. Well, I couldn't really do otherwise, could I? It would have complicated matters no end. I also cycled to the Mersey ferry terminal, and crossed the river to Liverpool. Leaving the next day I cycled to Nottingham, staying with a fellow T.O. (Tent Officer) whom I had met the previous year at the Crusader camp, and whose offer of accommodation on my epic journey I now took up. The last full day of my tour would take me to North London, where I again stayed at the home of a friend. My only memory from that was awakening during the night having thrown my arm against the bedside lamp, and smashed the bulb, something I regret I did not confess to prior to departure., No doubt I got my just reward while cycling through Brixton, where I suffered my first and only puncture. Whilst attempting, dismally, to repair the puncture a man stopped by, and offered my a lift home in his very nice, big car (a Daimler, I believe). Why, I do not know to this day, but he took me almost to my front door, and I was able to cover the last few hundred yards on foot. A safe and lucky end to a very pleasant though arduous trip.

Brian at Waddington Way

At the start of November I received the call to join Her Majesty's Forces, and report to, of all places, *the Tower of London*. This was the home of the Royal Fusiliers, City of London regiment. A bus ride (or two) across the capital brought me to its front gates, and I now appreciated the feelings of those personages who, over the years, had been brought there for imprisonment and possible execution. Those first days were an experience, sleeping in barrack-like accommodation with thirty or so other recruits, and getting used to the rough and ill-fitting khaki uniform. Beds were stripped down each morning, and then regimentally re-made for inspection. Toilet articles also had to be laid out, whilst clothing within the lockers not only had to be tidied but also box-edged with the aid of cardboard. And those boots....it was a major task to convert them into highly-shined objects with the aid of boot polish and a hot spoon. Soap was used to aid the formation in the correct places of sharp creases in the uniforms, and much time was spent in blanco-ing webbing and polishing brasses. Any other "spare" time was accounted for by buffing the living-area floors till they shone like mirrors, and oh yes, drilling and marching, and carrying out weapons exercises. All this in the once-moated area of the Tower, and where one could be seen – and criticized – by any passing member of the public.

There were of course moments of levity – of a sort. At our first medical parade we all had to receive injections. Next to me in the queue was a huge East-Ender who had bragged that he was not afraid of anything and that, as a boxer, he was going to enjoy his time in the army. He might well have done, but just before going in to see the M.O. he fainted clean away. The thought of a needle in his arm had made him keel over. Then there was the recruit who went home on leave in his uniform, and returned, having drunk well and remembered less well, in his civvies. A funny sight indeed next morning on parade! Oh yes, we did have the odd week-end pass out, but in the main it was only the local lads who took them…it took too long for the others to get home and back again. And, of course, there was the inevitable homesickness to be coped with, with and without leave.

The time came at last for us to be posted to our "proper" battalions…the Fusiliers was for many of us just the Basic Training posting. I had been selected as potential officer material (ha!) and was sent down to Canterbury, to join the Royal East Kent Regiment…..the Buffs. Here things would be different, and how! First, of course, the colour of the blanco changed, so that kept us busy for a while. Also, there was the cap badge and the arm flashes, all to be changed over. There were new colleagues to get to know, and a new Platoon Sergeant to get to know us. Then there were the lectures we had to attend, some about battle tactics, some about weaponry and others about army life in general. We were after all preparing to become officers, and to lead others into battle. The weather too was nothing to write home about, and at the end of one home leave, the fog was so thick that Sunday afternoon it seemed that I would not make it back to Base. Dad took me to Gipsy Hill railway station, but the trains had stopped running, so we went on to Catford, where I was lucky to catch a Green Line coach to Canterbury. How I got to the actual camp I have now no idea. Others had not been so lucky, and were subject to the "you should have left earlier" routine, plus a spot of fatigues.

Rifle practice at the Butts was fun, spraying the Sten gun around even more so, and dismantling and re-assembling the Bren machine gun proved challenging. The physical side of army life too was at first a challenge, then a bore and then – in my case anyway – a proper pain. I could cope with the assault course training, and bayonet practice and unarmed combat were opportunities for us to let off a bit of steam, but I was less enamoured with the cross-country runs, usually early morning and before breakfast in the NAAFI canteen. Eventually, persistent blisters on both heels led to being "excused boots", and - despite creditable showings in most activities, I had been unable to fulfill the training regime as it should have been. So, at least I was excused the chance to fail the OCTU selection held in Chester; I was in fact excused the opportunity to even try it out at all. Before the end of the course was reached, I was given the chance to re-direct my talents to another area and, as

I wished eventually to follow a teaching career after the army, opted for the R.A.E.C (Education Corps).

So, after a spot of home leave, I joined my new posting at Beaconsfield for a twelve-week course. The Corps was housed in an old country house and estate, outside the town. It was now the Spring of 1953, although it was late in announcing itself that year. The weather was cold and wet and we were still subject at times to square-bashing and rifle practice. It was here that I experienced the apocryphal story about whitewashing anything that didn't move, including the coal. Fortunately there was not much of that around and the Nissan huts too - both for living in and for training - were cold, as fuel for the central stoves was hard to come by. My parents had already moved home, preparatory to a final move to Spain, and were living in a two-bed apartment in Dulwich, South London. Their heating too was solid fuel, which at the time was proving more and more difficult to obtain. And then came the East Coast floods; one of our lot was sent home without warning to Mablethorpe, where it seemed that his family was in dire straits. However, the end of the training period eventually arrived, and we were called in one by one to be told of our eventual overseas posting…Germany, or the Far East, with the rank of Sergeant in the Education Corps.

The good news was that I had been given a "home" posting – to Germany., The bad news was that I needed a pass in Mathematics to even enter the RAEC, and that this had been overlooked. Impasse! It was eventually decided that I should sit the army's First Class Certificate of Education and, if I passed, the position would be reviewed. I did, and it was, but by that time I had missed that draft, and was seconded to the next one….to the Far East. Germany's loss, but definitely my gain. In what seemed no time at all I was kitted out in jungle green – very smart tunic top and shorts, jungle green underwear, and ankle webbing (to stop the snakes climbing our legs, we were told! And jungle green webbing – belt and ammo pouches – which would NOT (praise be!) require blancoing. We did however retain our usual battledress, but the stripes and new flashes (showing palm trees) would have to be sewn on, and after another short spell of home leave I reported in full uniform to Southampton Docks to join the S.S. Empire Pride.

As the troopship pulled away I confess to a feeling of trepidation. After all, at the tender age of nineteen I was about to be carted off to the other side of the world to do and see what I had no inkling. Passage through the Channel and into the Bay of Biscay was uneventful, but on passing through the Straits of Gibraltar and into the Mediterranean one could not help but think that the last tie with England was being broken. At last we arrived at Aden; "bumboats" laden with fabrics, pottery and souvenirs swarmed about the ship, with long-gowned men shouting their wares. If anyone showed even the slightest interest a rope would be thrown up with a basket containing some exotic item or other attached to be drawn up. Money then travelled the other way. Little boys in the water also performed, swimming and diving for coins thrown to them. They seemed to miss very few. All around there was a frenetic activity, as we were by far not the only ship in harbour, and it was a relief to change into civvies and take the boat to the quayside for as few hours of sightseeing and shopping. Not that there was much there to see, as the main town lay too far from the harbour to access easily. I did, however, purchase a very smart gold wristwatch, which I proudly displayed to all and sundry once back on board. Little did I know then that by the end of the journey the salt sea air would have begun its work, and that the "gold" covering would have peeled off. Ah well, one lives and learns, so they say.

On leaving Aden behind the ship entered the Suez Canal, alongside which could be seen small habitations, with donkeys providing the more common form of transport. Once we passed an army outpost, with suntanned soldiery standing guard outside. "Get your knees brown" would come the cry and, whilst we may have envied them their colouring, that particular posting did not seem too attractive. Travel across the Indian Ocean was another thing altogether. The ship was a veritable cattleboat, constructed mainly of steel, and reflected the heat, and we were permitted at last to strip off our battledresses and lie about in our jungle-green shorts. The sun blazed down, the flying fish flew and the dolphins followed, waiting for their meals to be thrown overboard once we had finished ours. The nights too were so warm that we were permitted to sleep on deck throughout the week that it took us to reach Ceylon and our next port of call. Three incidents stand out in my mind. First, I developed toothache, and had to have a molar removed by the ship's butcher...sorry, dentist. Then, overcome by the daytime heat, I managed to get a rather bad case of sunburn. Under normal circumstances, if this had prevented attending for duty, it would have been cause for disciplinary action, but as there was little to do in any case I got away with it. And thirdly,..ah yes, those were the days. Two of our sergeants were apprehended in homosexual activity, arrested, reduced to the ranks and were to be sent home in disgrace from Colombo That taught 'em...and the rest of us too, no doubt.

On arrival at the port there was the usual general exodus from the ship which, this time, I could not join in. I had drawn the duty of Orderly Sergeant, which meant remaining on board, seeing to the discipline and well-being of its occupants (certainly those returning from an afternoon's drinking ashore) and being a general dogsbody. The next day we were to sail between the island of Sumatra and the mainland of Malaysia, to arrive eventually at the mysterious island city of Singapore. We were also to learn for the first time of our ultimate destination; would it be a posting to Malaya, to Singapore or even to Hong Kong? I had loosely teamed up with another RAEC sergeant during the journey, but here our ways were to separate ..he was going on to Hong Kong, whilst I was to stay – somewhere – on the island of Singapore. A four-tonner awaited us at the docks, and a number of us were transported to our new but temporary accommodation, at the REME Rowcroft Lines. We were back to Nissan huts, but this time with mosquito netting, and with little to do but await notification of our eventual posting, to H.Q. Singapore City or upcountry into Malaya. Meantime we were granted associate membership of the Sergeants' Mess, and experienced for the first time the regimen of such an establishment. It was fortunate indeed, I thought, that I had NOT been accepted for OCTU training….I could not have afforded to have become an officer!

Doris Mabel Davies – A Biography

Born 27th March 1908 in South Wales, Doris was one of three daughters. Her father was a captain in the merchant navy and her mother was the village post mistress and local church organist. She graduated from Swansea University with a 1st Class Honours degree in history and commenced her teaching career in 1931 in Neath, South Wales. Here, she met Gwilym, who always called her "Dolly" and this name remained with her for the rest of her life. They became engaged and after a couple of years she followed Gwilym to London where he was a junior police officer and they got married. Dolly gave up teaching for about five years, during which time she bore two sons, first Brian, and then Colin two years later. She recommenced her teaching career just before the start of the Second World War and both she and Gwilym continued to live in London throughout the war and the bombing, although the children were evacuated to South Wales.

In London with the Andersen Shelter

She had many organising skills and was particularly interested in English Literature and drama and she took pleasure in producing a number of school plays. She also wrote a long novel on the lines of "How Green Was My Valley".

Unfortunately it was never published, but nevertheless it was highly praised.

Doris Mabel Davies

She and Gwilym were great travellers and were brave enough to go motoring in France and Spain as long ago as 1948. In those days, if you saw another British car approaching, you would flash your headlights and wave furiously, but it was a rare occurrence. Even after Gwilym died, Dolly loved to come on family holidays and even managed to fit in a few trips to Spain, as well as to Madeira and Malta on her own.

In spite of her commitment to her career, she found time to be a loving and caring mother. She was scrupulously fair and would go out of her way to ensure that her children were treated equally on absolutely ever occasion. She was also extremely generous and would frequently go without something herself in order that her children could benefit, but she never complained, and she never had a bad word to say about anyone, however great the provocation.

She continued teaching full time, gradually progressing up the ladder so that, by the time she retired, she had reached deputy head mistress. Her retirement was in fact premature, as she and Gwilym had decided to go to live in Spain, having fallen in love with the place during previous holidays. They chose a plot of what can only be described as desert, on the side of a hill and proceeded to build a magnificent house and transform the hillside into a beautiful garden with glorious views of the Mediterranean.

Mar-y-Sierra, Spain

Dolly had a great love of cats which she was able to indulge freely in Spain and soon all the strays in the neighbourhood seemed to know about the soft English couple living in the hills.

Their cats in Spain

Gwilym and Dolly on the steps of Mar-y-Sierra, Spain

After fourteen years, which were not without their tribulations, Gwilym's health deteriorated and they sold up and returned to England to live in Oundle. Gwilym's health continued to fail and after his death in 1982 Dolly moved to Croydon so that Colin and Mickie could keep an eye on her. At that time, she regularly attended Saint John's with Mickie, returning to join the family for a Sunday roast lunch. Dolly derived great pleasure from her four grandchildren; first Jonathan, then Bethan, followed somewhat later by Geraint and Howard. She always showed a great interest in their achievements and was in turn much loved by them all. We all miss her very much.

At home in Croydon in the late 1980s

Doris Mabel Davies – Notes About Her Life

Doris was born in Treherbert, South Wales, at 24 Miskin Street, on 27th March 1908.

Her parents were Edward Phillips and Mabel Davies, and she had two sisters, Muriel, born in 1910, and Olga born 1914. They lived at the Post Office in Giants Grave.

Mabel's mother was Charlotte Davies (nee Johns), who had held the position of postmistress there, and eventually Mabel succeeded her. She was later followed by her youngest daughter Olga, after the Post Office had moved to Brynhyfred.

Doris went to primary (Junior) School at Brynhyfred. When she left the school she travelled to the Grammar School in Neath, from which she gained entry to Swansea University. Here she obtained a degree in English in 1929, a B.A. Hon. in 1930 and a Teachers Diploma in 1931 Doris began her teaching career between 1931-32 at Court Sart Central in Neath, but transferred to West Heathly C.E. school in Sussex. She then returned home and taught at Brynhyfred School, Giants Grave between 1932-33. During this period she had met her future husband, Gwilym Davies of Neath. Looking for a career, Gwilym moved to London and joined the Metropolitan Police force. Doris visited (and stayed with) Gwilym at his lodgings in Greenwich for Christmas 1932, where their son Brian was conceived. As a result Doris returned to London to marry Gwilym at Poplar Register Office in June 1933, and became a full-time mother in September. Their second son Colin was born in February 1936.

Between 1938 and 1940 Doris became a Supply Teacher with the L.C.C., moving to Fortescue Secondary School in Mitcham in 1941. Having completed her permanent probationary year, Doris was in 1942 awarded her Teaching Certificate. In 1956, having worked as Acting Head on the retirement of the Headmistress, Doris moved school to Wandsworth Secondary Technical School. This was followed in 1958 by a transfer to Collingwood Secondary School in Peckham, where she became Deputy Head. She retired in 1961 and she and Gwilym emigrated to Spain, building and living in their villa near to Fuengirola on the Costa del Sol. Gwilym's poor health forced their return to the U.K. in 1978, and they moved to Oundle to be near to Brian and family. After Gwilym's death in 1982 Doris moved to the Croydon area of South London to live near Colin. In 1993 she became infirm enough to need to move into a nursing home in Caterham, Surrey where she died on 4th January 1994.

During the War Years Doris and Gwilym lived in Sydenham, South London. From here she travelled by bus and underground to her school, leaving home early and getting back late, and experienced both her bus being machine-gunned and her home bombed. Due to this, they moved Colin to live with his paternal grandparents in Neath, whilst Brian – after a one-year spell as an evacuee in Cwmgrach - a South Wales valley village - was in 1941 sent to the Kings School in Ely, Cambridgeshire for the remainder of the war. Gwilym as a police constable was working shifts and also studying for promotion, so Doris took the opportunity to write a semi-autobiographical book called "For Sufferance is the Badge" and which is yet (hopefully) to be published.

Colin's Life Story – Part 1
1939 to 1945

NEATH

I was evacuated to live with my grandparents in Neath sometime between 1939 and September 1940 when the Blitz started. When I say "evacuated", I think in reality my grandfather came by train from Neath to Paddington station to collect me. He was a railway worker in Neath, so it would not have cost him anything.

There are photographs of children queuing at railway stations, wearing name labels and carrying cardboard boxes holding their gas masks, but that wasn't me.

From that time on, I lived more or less continually at 13 Creswell Road until the end of the war.

In my opinion, we lived in comparative poverty, myself Dada John, Gramma Sarah and "uncle" Will.

Gramma Sarah and Dada John

I use the word advisedly because we were not actually poor. Uncle Will worked as a brickie at the Port Talbot steel works and Dada John was a railway worker at the marshalling yards in Neath, part of the Great Western Railway. On top of that, "Gramma" was a skilled seamstress and she regularly went out to clients locally, altering and making clothes. Finally of course, one would like to think that my parents (Doris & Gwilym) were also in a position to contribute to my welfare. Dad was a police officer in London and Doris was a school teacher.

Nevertheless we still lived in conditions of poverty, both physically and mentally and I will try to explain why!
When I arrived, I was given the front double bedroom overlooking the street. There was a large double bed with
(I was reliably told) a feather bed. Also a wash stand, a chest of drawers and a wardrobe. Uncle Will occupied the single room over the downstairs hallway and passage and my grandparents had the back bedroom looking over the yard. It wasn't a back garden as such, because it was dominated by a large shed which my uncle used as an aviary for his collection of canaries. On the other side of the pathway was the hen house and chicken run covered in wire netting. There was also a narrow room on a half landing and over the kitchen. This was called the office but in reality was where my grandmother had her sewing machine in front of the window. The poor woman was riddled with rheumatoid arthritis for as long as I remember and had to use the palm of her hand rather than her fingers to operate the machine. No electricity of course, so it was driven by foot treadle. Goodness knows how she managed to thread her needles, but she did.

Downstairs and to the left, off the front passage was the Front Room, furnished in the main by a three piece suite surrounded by cabinets and glass covered displays of stuffed birds, stoats and other animals! There was a table in the middle of the room and the only time this room was ever used was when there was a funeral, or if the Minister called of course. Next down the passage and at the bottom of the staircase was the Middle Room. This had a large sideboard, a leather sofa and a table &

chairs and was where Uncle Will lived. There was a wooden cabinet with on top the Relay Radio. Just a loudspeaker really. It was connected by cable and as far as I know only received the BBC Home Service! My grandparents paid a few pence each week to a firm called funnily enough "Radio Rentals".

To the right was a cupboard under the stairs and at one time an Alsatian dog called Jack lived here. I recall him being commanded to "go to cwtch" periodically but I never saw him being walked anywhere at all. Perhaps he was just a figment of my imagination!

Once in the kitchen, you would find immediately to the right a food cupboard and next to it the cast iron gas stove.

Opposite was the back door leading to the back yard. Next to the gas stove was a leather sofa then a wooden armchair and at the far end the fireplace. This is where my grandfather reigned supreme, chain smoking his pipe and clearing the phlegm in his throat from time to time before disgorging it into the fire with a hiss. Except when he missed of course. On the mantelpiece above the fireplace were the ubiquitous Staffordshire dogs, one each side standing guard and on the wall above there was a gas light.

On the left side of the room was the kitchen window with a wooden table in front. This table was used for everything, from holding the Littlewoods pools coupons each Saturday while Dada checked the results from the radio, to food preparation and of course dining. I have a strong recollection of my grandfather preparing a salad. He used a chopping board and bunched the lettuce and shibbons together whilst slicing with a sharp knife. He would then slice them in the other direction and then chop, chop, chop until everything was reduced to miniscule proportions.

Boiled egg would be added as we had chickens of course, and finally everything would be added to a large glass bowl and stirred up again, possibly with seasoning and small chunks of Cheddar cheese. It never occurred to me at the time, but possibly this was the only way my grandparents could enjoy a green salad because of their dentures!

But I digress. Doubtless you will notice that I have not mentioned the bathroom. That is because there wasn't one! In the back yard there was admittedly an outside W.C and a standpipe nearby supplying copious amounts of cold water. If you wanted a wash, you had to part fill a bowl and take it into the kitchen then boil up the kettle.

Being war time, there was no proper toilet paper. Just torn up strips of the Western Mail. This was perhaps fortuitous as there was not much other reading matter available as I can recall. (It is fair to say that relations like Nanny in Briton Ferry and some friends had a roll of proper toilet paper in their bathrooms).

There were the inevitable religious books such as the Bible of course and numerous hymn and prayer books. Also a copy of Old Moore's Almanac. I used to borrow comics from my friends, in particular from David Evans. His father was a solicitor and they lived in a big house in Beechwood Avenue.

I did have some children's books of course such as Babar the Elephant and his mother Queen Celeste. Also Winnie The Pooh and the Tales of Brer Rabbit.

I had a few large wooden toys including a red painted railway engine and a wooden bus with detachable lid.

My Uncle Will and grandparents would normally converse in Welsh which was impossible for me to understand, so to a large extent I lived an isolated and miserable existence. They didn't do it on purpose I'm sure, but they just didn't think anything about the consequences. I remember when meeting other grown-ups, I was always described as very quiet and well behaved. That was how my father liked his children to be, so doubtless it was a family trait!

I also recall some years later that I was described as talking with a plum in my mouth and I was even given elocution lessons at school.

My grandparents were very devout Methodists and I was strictly forbidden to whistle on a Sunday. This was ironic as in the front window was a large coloured statue of the very popular "Whistling Boy". Every Sunday morning, my Grandparents would walk along Eastland Road to the Methodist Chapel. For some unknown reason, I was dispatched to Bethania Chapel at the bottom of Creswell Road, a mere fifty yards away. Here I would sit in a pew, closed in by a small door and spend an hour or more listening to a sermon and attempting to join in singing hymns all completely in Welsh. What an utter waste of time! They might as well have shut me in the cupboard under the stairs with the dog!

I went to the Gnoll school and my first primary school teacher was a nice sympathetic lady we called Miss Parsons.
I stayed for school dinners each day, even though home was only five minutes' walk away. I never really enjoyed faggots and peas, but I don't suppose it did me any harm.
Apart from David Evans, I had two other close friends at school. Michael Jones was the Minister's son and they lived in Woodland Avenue. Their house was large, very dark and smelled strongly of furniture polish. His mother was a gorgeous platinum blonde! My other friend was called Alan Webley and he lived in Eastland Road. I don't remember much about him other than the fact that he had a Meccano set. This he had used to build a large model of Tower Bridge. We spent a lot of time together making modifications between us.
One of the disadvantages of not having a bathroom was that hygiene was never a priority. Probably having newspaper instead of proper toilet tissue also contributed to this problem! One day I was detained at school and given multiple showers with copious amounts of carbolic soap. These showers were followed by sessions with a sun lamp, so I guess I must have been suffering from a lack of vitamin D as well. Nobody ever bothered to explain to me at such a young age and I probably would not have understood anyway.
We were extremely blessed in many ways, because apart from the Baptist Chapel at the bottom of Creswell Road,
in Eastland Road at the other end lived a dentist! Most adults must have had dentures in those days, because that was another subject I knew absolutely nothing about. Until I developed tooth ache that is! I suppose I owned a tooth brush but it was war-time, as I have already mentioned. I did enjoy sweets, but they were rationed of course. There was a sweet shop on the corner of Greenway Road and I particularly liked liquorice sticks which used to stain tongue, lips and teeth a horrible black colour. On the corner of Creswell Road was Gormans, a general store and Mr Gorman wore a brown overall .
On the other side of the road, down Rope Walk, was our closest fish & chip shop. I used to be sent here quite regularly

to purchase fish and chips wrapped possibly in the Western Mail again!

Nearby was the doctor's surgery with the dispensary attached. I didn't need to go here very often, fortunately, but one morning I woke on my feather bed with excruciating tummy ache.(My brother says it differently…that HE and I were sent home from school, each with a tummy ache, but his were only sympathetic pains!! I don't remember him being there at all.) I was rushed by ambulance to Penrhiwtyn hospital where apparently I had developed peritonitis caused by a burst appendix. After the operation, I was thrilled to have a visit from my parents who had rushed down from London. According to my father, I took one look at them and said "go away", but at the tender age of five and given all the circumstances, who can blame me!

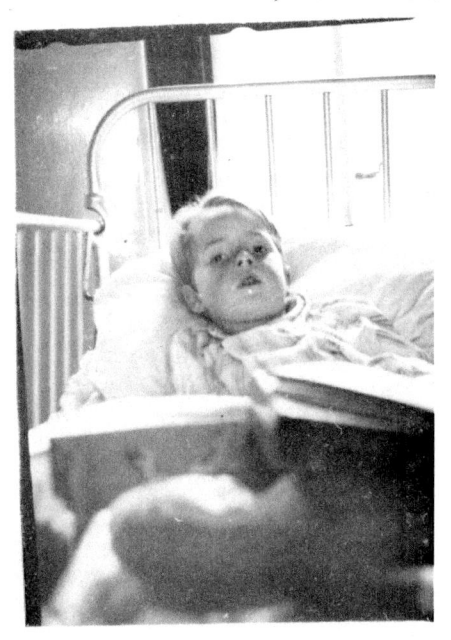

Colin in hospital, May 1940

I can still recall two events from that harrowing time. One was having ether dripped onto a mask prior to intubation. The second was the removal of the clamps when my scar had healed . I have only to look at my stomach in the mirror, to be reminded of that horrible experience!

I have mentioned before that we did not have any electricity, so when it became too dark to read, I would listen to the radio. The gas lamp in the middle room and kitchen were lit then with a taper. The lights outside in the street were gas too and these were also ignited by a lamplighter walking up and down the street with a long pole.

Being war-time, the hourly news was a favourite subject, but I also had an opportunity to listen to Children's Hour. Uncle Mac, (Derek McCulloch) was the presenter and was famous for his signoff "Good night Children everywhere".

The other unforgettable programme was Toytown, featuring Larry the Lamb and Ernest the Dachshund.

I enjoyed the various music programmes with songs like "Don't sit under the apple tree with anyone else but me", sung by the Andrew Sisters. Then there was the indefatigable Vera Lynn of course with "The white cliffs of Dover".

During the day the milk was delivered regularly by the local dairy farm in giant silver coloured milk churns. The milk cart was pulled by one if not two cart horses and as he turned into the street, all the housewives appeared on their respective door steps armed with an empty milk jug. Sometimes two if there was a large family inside. The milkman had a dibber with a brass handle and he dipped this into the churn before upending the contents into each waiting jug. There were no such things as refrigerators in those days, so folks only bought sufficient for their daily needs.

Bread was also delivered in a similar manner but the most exciting delivery of all was the rag and bone man!

He announced his arrival with a huge bell and his raucous street call. He didn't pay for the old clothes or metal he collected but sometimes if you were lucky you might get a goldfish or a rubbing stone. These stones were used by the housewives to scrub their doorsteps clean and woe betide you if you ever stepped on one that had just been done!.

It is a surprise how any traffic managed to pass through Creswell Road at all, because there were also horse and carts delivering bags of coal, deliveries of oil and paraffin and even the occasional knife sharpener. with a circular grindstone operated by a treadle. It has to be remembered however that not a single motor vehicle was parked outside any of the properties, as car ownership was a luxury in those days and petrol was rationed as well.

Life didn't just revolve around Creswell Road of course and I spent much time the other side of Eastland Road walking up Gnoll Drive to the brook. This was a shallow stream where together with various pals, we collected tadpoles in jam jars and generally fell in the water and got into trouble afterwards. It was comparatively safe to play in the street as well, but sometimes we got shouted at for bouncing a ball against somebody's front door or house facade.

Victoria Gardens were close by, not much fun as there were keep off the grass signs everywhere and park keepers who were not averse to giving chase if the mood took them.

My mother's family lived a short bus ride away in Giant's Grave, Briton Ferry. If you took the bus for the Old Road, it crossed the main road by the Lodge Cinema and continued over the railway bridge before climbing the steep hill to Elm Road. Here it stopped for a short while to get its breath back, before continuing down to the rail bridge again.

A short walk downhill from the stop on Elm Road was Giant's Grave Road and the post office run by my grandmother Mrs Mabel Philips. Her husband (Eddie) was a retired sea captain and I saw little of him. Mabel's youngest daughter Olga also lived in the house with her husband Cecil who was in the RAF. They had one son, Basil who might possibly have been born a year after me. I never got to know him very well. He had been spending quite a lot of time with a Mr Watkins nearby and it was young Basil who taught me my first swear word ....BUGGER!

I had another cousin who was a year older than me and lived with her parents, Wilfred & Muriel at a grocery store at the bottom of Giant's Grave Road, opposite the cemetery. Joan was very sophisticated and sometimes gave me the impression she couldn't be bothered with such small fry! Nevertheless I enjoyed her company and was happy to tag along whenever I could. The back garden of the property consisted of a narrow yard area with a raised bed against the wall to the road. This was decorated with numerous concrete faces using sea shells for the features. A little bit like a miniature version of the figures on Easter Island. I never did find out who was responsible for them.

At the bottom of the road was Wards Breakers Yard, where old ships were broken up for scrap metal. This was where my Uncle Gordon worked, down by the canal.

Occasionally my Uncle Will took me by train to Porthcawl. Here was a large fairground and I had fun on the ghost train and various rides and attractions. Afterwards he took me to a cafe where I had a knickerbocker glory. Oh joy!

One BBC program called it the 'dessert of childhood dreams'!

Which brings me nicely to Irene McBurney who lived across on the other side of Creswell Road. Her parents were Italian but not approved of by my grandparents. For a farthing, Irene was happy to show you her sights!

At some stage, so let us guess, when I was about seven or eight, my Uncle Will started courting Dinah. She was a waitress at a local restaurant. It must have been a quiet wedding because I don't remember it. I do remember that I had to give up my comfortable feather bed and matching pillows and move into the small front bedroom previously occupied by my Uncle.

So Auntie Dinah moved into my life and continued to live in the middle room. To be fair, she did try to make a fuss of me and spoil me, realising that I may have had my nose put out of joint just a little. She was a more adventurous cook than either of my grandparents and would conjure up a plate of gammon, egg and chips on the small cast iron stove in the kitchen. It put a lot of pressure on the facilities but we all managed to get along.

As I mentioned before, the war years were a time of hardship and rationing, but I know for a fact that my grandparents passed on to me a lot of their entitlement. Another good thing about Dinah was that being closer to my parent's age, she was happy to become a sort of surrogate mother to me and although she still spoke in Welsh to my grandparents, I no longer felt isolated.

She sometimes had a visitor she called Uncle Beynon. I don't know whether he was a friend or a relation, but he was good for a half crown every time he called, so who was I to complain.

I mentioned earlier that my Dada smoked a pipe continually when he was not out working on the railway.

Uncle Will by contrast was a Woodbine fan and inevitably there was a fag hanging from his lower lip at any time of the day. Poor Dinah was an asthma sufferer, but I never heard her complain. Willie also was a keen billiards fan and used to spend a lot of his free time down at the billiard hall near the station.

So it was a wonder how I ever managed to avoid suffering from the effects of secondary smoking during the years I spent living in Neath. But more on that later.

I had an uncle John living in Glyncorrwg. He was a coal miner and he worked in the local colliery. He once arranged for me to visit the colliery with him and I was amazed how men could live and work in those conditions.

He had married Auntie Mary who was I believe his second wife. Their privy was even further down their garden, backing on to a stream, so I tried to avoid calling as much as possible. It was a wooden bench seat with a hole in it rather than the normal bowl.

Can't remember about the paper!

John was a big noisy man but he had a heart of gold and once gifted me a half sovereign, possibly from his stash under the mattress. Mary was a tidy little thing and obviously adored him. She went to a lot of trouble giving me cheese and shibbons from their vegetable patch if I were to visit.

I do remember that once the war in Europe was over, we had a street party in Creswell Road. The date was May 1945. Lots of pop and fish paste sandwiches I would imagine. Who knows?

On VJ day when the Japanese capitulated, finally the war was really over and we had another street party!

What I do know is that some time later in September 1945 I was back living with Mum & Dad again (and my elder brother Brian), this time in Waddington Way, Upper Norwood, Croydon.

Colin Wynne-Davies

Colin's Life Story – Part 2
From August 1952

In August 1952, when I was awaiting my 'O' Level results, I travelled by car to Innsbruck in Austria with Mum & Dad.
We stayed in the Gastzimmer at the police station courtesy of Dad's friend, the chief of police.
I recall that although our hospitality was free of charge, we still couldn't afford to go out for a meal twice a day. So Dad got his paraffin stove out of the car and we cooked lunch in the middle of the bedroom floor! Afterwards we had to leave all the windows open in order to try to get rid of the cooking smells!
Sometime during the holiday, my exam results were declared and somebody must have opened the post and phoned us the news. Not brilliant but not too bad. Except for French that is!

Colin aged 16 in 1952

Colin and his mother, Dolly, at Waddington Way

August 1953. Because Dad was based at Adelaide House, London Bridge, he worked closely with the immigration officers at the Port of London. He regularly used to enjoy a drink with his colleagues on the various ships in the docks and became friendly with Arthur French who was the company secretary of the Euxine shipping company with the head office in London. They owned two similar ships of just over 2,000 tons, the Hendi and the Helka. I don't know how it came about, but Mr French kindly arranged for me to travel as a supernumerary on one of their ships, the Helka, berthed at Hays Warf near London Bridge and Dad had requested the chief steward to keep an eye on me.

There were only a few official passengers including a Dutch lady friend of the owner (a Mrs DeJong) travelling with her teenage son & daughter.

So strictly speaking I was classed as a crew member and spent most of my free time drinking Grants whiskey and playing cribbage with some of the catering crew.

The journey was uneventful until we got to the Mediterranean, when we called at a port called Souse in Tunisia.

I recall leaving the ship for an evening stroll around the port. When I got back to the bottom of the gangway, a rather plump greasy looking Arab stopped me to check my passport. He was smoking a cheroot with one hand, but with his free hand he rubbed my tummy and indicated how he would like to know me better. I can tell you that I was up that gangway quicker than you could say djellaba and firmly locked inside my cabin!

Our captain was a Mr Wilkes and when we arrived at our next port of call, Alexandria, he arranged one day for us to visit the port agent, a Mr McRae. Mr McRae was a large Greek physically rather similar to Sydney Greenstreet the film actor. He had a beautiful Romanian wife and two children. Yvette about the same age as myself and her younger brother Nicky.

They lived in a gorgeous villa named Eleusis in Alexandria with servants and a chauffered company car. I was rather taken with Yvette and we arranged to write to each other later, as she spoke excellent English.

After a few days, we sailed on to Beirut in the Lebanon where one night the chief steward showed me around some of less salubrious areas around the port. Very much a question of look but don't touch I'm pleased to say!

The following day the captain and Mrs De Jong and family had arranged a taxi trip to Damascus about 2 hours drive away. I was most surprised to be invited as well and accepted with alacrity. The journey across the desert was painfully slow and we were constantly having to stop and show our papers at various military check-points along the way. Eventually we arrived in Damascus where the ubiquitous guide was waiting to escort us and show us the sights.

I spent quite a lot of my time in the Souqs and the Old City where I was able to do some shopping. A damask tablecloth, some embroidered cloths with silver thread as well as the usual tourist rubbish. Anyway I had a very interesting time and all too soon it was time to find our taxis and return to the ship.

We made one final call on the way home which was Antwerp. Can't remember much sight-seeing, but once again the chief steward took me around the bars where I had my first taste of Sweet Martini.

Then we were sailing back to England or so I thought. But the captain announced a change of plan & told me we were going to a place called Methil in Scotland. It is a tiny port near Kircaldy and I was little prepared to be unceremoniously dumped overboard, burdened as I was with two enormous leather hold-alls.

(I think we were given these by our next door neighbour Mr Bogart along with other items from his time in the Mediterranean as well as an assortment of wooden shafted golf clubs).

One was full of school books which I confess I never got round to reading and the other a collection of clothes mostly also unused because of the heat.

Anyway, by hook or by crook I finally made it back to London by train. No credit cards in those days, so I must have had a stash or notes rolled up in my sock or somewhere!

Over the following months, Yvette and I wrote to each other regularly and early in 1954, I received an invitation to spend my summer holidays in Alexandria. Needless to say, it was an opportunity of a lifetime, but I never expected it to come to fruition. It obviously involved some jiggling of dates and I had to leave school well before the end of the summer term in order to fit in with the sailing schedules.

I travelled on the Hendi this time under the captaincy of a Mr Ross. A very dour scotsman indeed. It was about a ten day run from Hay's wharf to Alex, so once we entered the Mediterranean, Captain Ross commanded his crew to build a framework of timber between the bulwarks and the superstructure on the main deck. This was covered with an immense tarpaulin and sea water was pumped in for what seemed hours. Eventually we had quite a respectable plunge pool, although only for the use of officers of course. My most memorable recollection is when I arrived one morning to find captain Ross sitting on the side with his feet in the water, stark naked! He had his willy in his hand and proceeded to pontificate about the many benefits of sunshine on one's private parts!

I was collected from the port in the company car and delivered once more to the Villa Eleusis where I was made welcome. Yvette had broken up from her school as well and the format appeared to be a breakfast of fruit followed by a trip to the Sidi Bishr beach. There is a Hilton Hotel there now, but nothing much but sand all those years ago.

Here I was introduced to a group of middle- class friends, mainly European but with a couple of Egyptians as well. Susi was a lovely Lebanese girl, and there was a Maltese and a Syrian girl as well. The local lads were really well built and strong swimmers and liked nothing better than to dive into the sea then swim through a submerged rock passage before coming up gasping for air in a deep pool. This was obviously to impress all the young ladies and although they tried to persuade me to attempt the same feat, I confess that I chickened out.

After the beach, we all met up in a local cafe drinking cola and listening to the Arab music.

When the temperature had dropped in the evening, we went back to the villa and dinner was served in their dining room.

A large table was covered with Egyptian linen and each of us had a large linen napkin neatly folded as in a restaurant.

I had only ever eaten in our kitchen before, so it was quite an experience. Silver service of course and a maid to clear away afterwards and do the washing up!

One evening I was tackling a delicious piece of fresh fish which naturally enough was full of bones. Mr McCrae complimented me with regard to my meticulous attention to detail and the precision with which I removed each offending bone. I replied that doubtless many hours in the biology lab dissecting frogs and dog fish had stood me in good stead.

After the meal, I thanked everybody and neatly folded up my linen napkin which seemed good enough to use again.

Mr McCrae moved very quickly for such a large man, reached across and crumpled it in his two hands. If you want to be invited back, he said, that's what you do with your napkin.

There was one other occasion when I fell foul of Yvette's father, but in a big way. At some time during my stay, Mr

French came to visit and offered to take me to Cairo to see the pyramids. Mr McCrae was concerned for my comfort and offered me some cigars to take for the journey. These I politely declined since I didn't smoke and had no wish to start. So then he pressed a half bottle of brandy upon me which I was unable to refuse. I travelled by train to Cairo first class with tables and fully reclining seats as well as air conditioning of course. The trip was most enjoyable and extremely interesting and somewhere there is a picture of me on a camel. On my return I was telling everyone about my adventure and then pulled the bottle of brandy out of my pocket and handed it back to Yvette's father!

Wow. He was furious. In my ignorance I had seriously insulted him and he said that I should have thrown it out the train window rather than return a gift. He didn't speak to me for days after that, but Mrs McCrae gradually talked him round.

Yvette was very slim and lightly built, unlike her buxom mother and huge father. At some stage she developed a chest infection with a nasty cough which wouldn't clear up. The doctor was called and I was invited into the parent's bedroom to view the treatment. There was a massive painting of a reclining nude on the wall behind the bed, so I knew where the Old Man's tastes lay!

Yvette was lying on her front on her parent's bed stripped to the waist and what looked like drinking glasses were being heated in a flame. Once hot, they were placed at various points on poor Yvette's back A process known as "cupping" therapy.

As they cooled, the air was sucked out causing the cups to stick to her back. It must have been most uncomfortable if not painful as she was crying bitterly.

I became quite pally with many of Yvette's friends over the holiday and one memorable day I was invited to join up with a group whose parents were members of the Royal Alexandria Yacht Club situated in the Grand harbour.

I say "Royal" because of King Farouk, but it had probably been renamed by then.

Anyway, there was a collection of small single-sailed wooden dinghies tied up and somebody suggested we borrow one and go for a sail! I think there was only enough room for three of us.

There was a brisk wind from the sea and we were soon skimming across the Grand harbour at a rate of knots.

Eventually, we thought it might be prudent to turn back but nobody knew the first thing about sailing!

We discovered how to stop by letting the sail go, but no way we could turn around to go back the way we came.

Fortunately the harbour was massive with very little traffic, but that also meant there was nobody we could ask for help. There were giant caissons about two metres across anchored in one area and we managed to grab hold of one and stop our headlong progress to God knows where! Then we just sat and waited hoping that somebody would miss us and send out a search party. This indeed happened eventually and three very subdued and contrite teenagers were towed back by the club launch!

King Farouk had been deposed in 1951 and it was still possible to visit his Ras-El-Tin palace, now stripped of valuables. In one of his bathrooms the bath was burnt & blackened where apparently he had burnt his documents and private papers before fleeing the country.

I suppose I must have been away from home for six weeks or more before the second of the Euxine Company ships called at Alexandria again to take me home.

The journey this time was uneventful with the exception that instead of a steward, we had a stewardess. She was a gorgeous blonde Norwegian young lady from the city of Bergen & I quickly forgot about Yvette and her family.

We did write to each other for a while and one day she phoned to say she had arrived in the Port of London.

Unfortunately Dad had answered the phone and he soon made it clear that there was no way we could meet up.

So that was that!

          Colin Wynne-Davies

Stories by Imogen Dudley
(age 9)

A CAT AND MOUSE TALE

Once upon a time there lived a small mouse called Minnie. She simply adored cheese, and stole cheese puffs from the larder. One day a cat came into the house and chased Minnie into a rat's mousehole. The rat was a very stroppy rat and she told Minnie to stop running into her house without knocking. Minnie said she was sorry and explained about the cat. The rat said "Oh!" and went outside her house and said "Oi, you cat, leave me and Minnie Mouse alone".

Then Minnie's *love* came in. "What's all the fuss about?" Then he saw Minnie and fainted. He got up and said "Bonjour, Ma'am, How can I help you?" "Well," she said "I would like it if this cat was destroyed, or even just scared." He thought for a moment and went to his mobile phone and called the Dog. The Dog said "O.K." and came and scared the cat away out of the house, and that was the end of the cat, for then, anyway.

THE END

THE PRINCESS AND THE TROLL

Once upon a time there lived a princess called Princess Clarabell. She lived in a small land called the Land of the Furies. Clarabell was once kidnapped and taken to the Troll's fort and she was stuck there for a hundred years. Then one day a handsome prince came; he was called Prince Gustavus. He had heard the tales of the princess and had come to rescue her. He had a rose in one hand and a sword in the other. He put a ladder against the wall. Just then the Troll came out. He growled and then went back inside. The Prince got out of his hiding place and began to climb up the castle, and saw the Princess asleep on the haystack. He picked her up and carried her down the ladder, but the Troll came out and chased them all the way to the Prince's castle. His army killed the Troll. Prince Gustavus and Princess Clarabell married and lived happily ever after.

THE END

Poems by Bethan K
(then a Teenager)

FIVE POEMS - by Bethan Kerensa Dudley (nee Davies)

REMEMBRANCE

There's a red glow through the window

Lighting up the sky;

You can hear the sirens wailing

And the anguished mother's cry

As her child's dragged from the building

And they say it's going to die.

The house is now a ruin,

The child and mother gone.

The village all deserted –

It's not the only one.

Possessions fade away in time

But memories linger on.

TO BE REBORN

To be reborn: that's my desire –

From such a life as this

And get the rebirth kiss.

To leave this life of which I tire

And be reborn to bliss.

But others found – who'd had a go –

The new's worse than the old.

So I'll just stick with what I know

And heed what I've been told.

THE DEPARTURE

The last time I had seen her she'd been fine,

Yet she must have known, because of the letter.

The letter sent some money, a present for Easter,

But it was only early February.

The next we heard she had left home.

Departed suddenly in the night.

Like a child who, on an impulse, runs away

Because it cannot cope with life at home.

Her mind could still cope, it was her body that fled

Away from this world with its everyday worries.

To a place more peaceful, where tired minds could rest.

She left home for the final time that night.

THE BODYGUARD

A handsome young man looking after another,

The other one older and very well-known.

The young one trained to look inconspicuous,

With a gun at his side - in case need arose.

A car behind them, An Alvis, speed twenty.

People watching from across the road.

The older is smiling, the younger is watching

As people pass by. He makes sure no-one tries

To harm his charge. He is good at his job.

FACES OF THE CITY

The man emerges from the pub

All battered and bleeding,

With a broken beer bottle in his hand.

He wears a look of hatred on his face

And, after taking a deep breath,

Turns and plunges once again

Into the depth of the fight.

A flashing blue light cuts through the darkness,

Four men jump out and someone yells "Scarper!"

The man with the broken bottle

Is dragged out, along with two of his companions.

The car drives off, and I move on.

        The tube train draws in

        And the doors are opened

        Two men force their way

        Through the crowds and out

        A woman pleads "Stop them –

        They've stolen my money".

But no-one comes to her aid.

People sit with their heads buried

Deep in their papers, or deep

In conversation with a friend.

All feel pity for her

But none wants to get involved.

This is one face of the city.

The face of crime and so-called

"Townies" who do even acknowledge

The existence of other people.

But there is another side – the excitement,

The sense of belonging.

In a village you may belong

To a small, discreet group,

But in the town you belong

To a huge club. No one knows

All the members, and yet they

Can all recognize each other.

Christmas

Footsteps in the snow, receding, leaving arrow-prints

Which show where we have been, where we have come from.

More footsteps, these advancing, coming towards us – I wonder

To where they will lead us over time? Ahead is Christmas,

A shining beacon of hope and joy, the children eagerly awaiting

Their unearned presents as their due. They have no knowledge

Of the past, only the future sparkles in their eyes.

Christmas in 1814, when the Thames froze, and skaters

Exhilarated, bonfires lit, and life for a short time

Brought hope to the many. The few already had expectation

For what their riches could bring.

The football match of 1914, when Christmas stopped the war

For a short time, bringing together foes who, a brief few minutes later,

Would seek to wipe each other from the earth's face.

Yet, what is Christmas without hope, without joy – the joy felt by

Mary and Joseph in the meanness of their stable home.

That hope that the world now savours as we seek to wipe the old year

From our memory, supplanting it by new ones as the old year withers.

The homeless in our streets, the disposessed in foreign lands,

All looking towards that bright new future…will it ever come?

Ah, regrets! It is too late now to reach out for what might have been;

Instead, embrace this Christmas as no other.

Embrace the tree which glistens even as it encourages us

To replace lost lives, lost loves, lost opportunities…lost everything!

And look ahead, even to Christmases yet to come.

                         Brian G Davies

Coming Home – A Hymn

COMING HOME

Jesus is listening, loving us

As with a shepherd's care;

Guiding his flock from sinful ways,

Teaching the power of prayer.

Jesus is listening, will he hear

Voices to Heaven raised?

His arms enfold as we draw near,

His glorious name be praised.

Jesus is waiting, come to Him,

No longer turn away.

Nothing the world can offer you

Is worthy of delay.

Jesus is waiting to bestow

Salvation on each one;

Who follows Christ His love will know,

His heavenly will be done.

Jesus is asking for my word

That I will follow Him.

I'll march triumphant with my Lord

When this world's glories dim.

Jesus is asking – shall I say

Take me and make me Thine?

Thy cleansing blood brings love and hope

And perfect peace divine.

Jesus is coming, me to save,

He died at Calvary.

And when at last He comes again

I know He'll come for me.

Jesus is coming, wave the palms,

It was for me He died.

And when He takes me in His arms

I shall be purified.

Jesus has listened, did I say

He is my everything?

I'll wait no longer for that day,

My life to Him I'll bring.

Jesus is now my resting-place,

No longer will I roam.

So, as I march towards my Lord

I know I'm coming home.

Section B

Travel Articles

Land of the Breton

1990

It was to be Brittany this year. A few years back we had intended to visit this beautiful area of France, but poor weather had driven us further south. This time the weather was perfect as we disembarked from our ferry at St. Malo. Our passage with Brittany Ferries included a pre-booked first night's stay at Camping Bel Event, a 3-star site a few kilometres to the south-east , and a great site for our first night's rest after the 9-hour crossing from Portsmouth. Tomorrow we would be off, with but minor diversions, to the Gulf of Morbihan.

Dol de Bretagne, the picturesque capital of the Marais, is near enough not to miss. In the 12th century the sea washed the foot of the cliff on which it stands, dominated by the cathedral of St. Sampson. Today the main street, down which came the American army of liberation in 1944, contains an interesting motley of architectural styles. The shops themselves offer a wide variety of product and produce at prices not too far removed from those in the U.K.

The N176 took us south-west to Dinan, standing some 240 feet above the river Rance. Tourists and lorries alike climb laboriously into the medieval market place, where parking spaces were plentiful, though in great demand. The adjacent Old Quarter holds much for the tourist to see amongst its leaning ancient buildings. Of special note are the Barbican, the Clock Tower and the English Garden with its stupendous view over the river.

Our overnight stop was to be at Josselin. The municipal site just west of the town provided acres of well-tended and terraced space, with clean and adequate facilities.

It stands on the banks of the Oust canal, which links Nantes with Brest. A leisurely evening walk along the road takes one to the town's edge, where we encountered the famed cara-boats. These are seemingly flat-bottomed punts on to which have been loaded a small caravan – very comfortable and in great demand as canal pleasure boats. The return journey along the north bank made a total of just over an hour. Next morning we set down our camper in the car park at the water's edge (where there are toilets and free parking), while we inspected the huge ramparts and the trio of fairy towers of Josselin Chateau. In the town itself is the Musee de Poupees, with its 500 or so dolls from the Rohan family collection. If you are there in early September you may catch the religious procession, or Pardon, which many towns stage at some time during the year. Like most places in Brittany, we found everywhere to be clean and litter-free.

The journey's main destination was to be the city of Vannes in southern Brittany, and the area surrounding the Gulf of Morbihan, but we still had two calls to make before getting there. The first was at Ploemel, some 12 miles east of Josselin, where both car parking and flower beds abounded. Once the seat of the Dukes of Brittany, little now remains of the town's fortifications. It is also, however, famed as home to Doctor Guerin, inventor of the surgical dressing, in time for the Franco-Prussian war of 1870.

A few miles before Vannes we stopped at a picnic area on the edge of Elven. This, really a picnic/information/toilet/campsite combination, was ideal for a lunch break before tackling the big city. The young French student manning the information desk spoke excellent English; she took our photo, and provided us with a map of Vannes, and a wealth of detail on the local places of interest. Nearby at Malestroit is the Brittany museum of the Resistance. If you need to shop before arriving at your camp site you can do no better than to turn right (west) onto the N165 dual-carriageway towards Auray. Watch out for the "Continent" sign, turn off and cross above the roadway straight into the hypermarket's huge, but usually crowded car park. The complex is well served with a variety of shops but "Continent" will meet most of your needs. We stayed for over two hours, then made our way back towards Vannes itself. We turned off, however, onto the D780, and skirted the gulf until reaching its terminus at Port Navalo. The municipal site of Port Sable is right above the beach, with good facilities. It is also popular and can be pretty crowded, but from here one can watch the stream of small craft heading for the new marina.

One of the many residences of the Dukes of Brittany in past times was the Chateau of Suscinio, a medieval castle badly vandalised during the French Revolution. Check on times of opening before calling, as it is some way off the main road, but it is a visit not to be missed. From its towers there is a magnificent view seawards; the beach here has ample parking space with, however, a single tardis-like toilet. A swim to cool down, lunch, then we retraced our steps along the excellent road past Vannes to St. Anne d'Auray. Famous mainly as a place of pilgrimage it is like, Lourdes, crowded later in the day so earlier is best. Familiarise yourself with the legend, then visit the Basilica, the Sacred Steps and the War Memorial, and marvel at how much is built on a little faith. Although standing on a sixth-century site, the present building dates only from the mid-19th century.

The Carnac area is world-renowned for its burial chambers (dolmens) and standing stones (menhirs). However, some of the more impressive are to be found at Lochmariaque, at the entrance to the Gulf. Of especial interest is the Grand Menhir, once some 20 metres high, and thought to have been the main focus of an amazing astrological system stretching across the area. Unfortunately, having in the past been struck by lightning, it now lies on the ground, broken into four large sections. When you have at last exhausted the possibilities – and yourself – I can recommend the campsite of La Falaise to the west of the town and on the coast. Large but well-kept, and with a shop and excellent facilities, it is protected from the wind by the dunes, along the top of which runs the road. At high tide these provide ideal bathing conditions, dropping just steeply enough to permit a proper swim without the usual longish walk into the sea.

The approach to the port and sailing centre of Trinite-sur-Mer is impressive., the viaduct sloping gently down from east to west as it crosses the river Crach. Masts of all sizes proliferate, and Trinite is one of the oldest and largest ports in southern Brittany. Keep left, and you can park next to the quay, bear right and the road climbs out again to the megalithic complex of Carnac. Note especially the enormous tumulus of St. Michael, over 120 metres long and about 12 metres high, containing several chambers. Remains found in these date back some 4000 years. Just north of the town are the spectacular 'alignments' of Menac, twelve lines of over 1000 menhirs of various sizes. Other nearby alignments may well have been linked at some time, but the exact purpose of these gigantic works remains a mystery.

Take the road west to Plouharmel and here turn off towards Presqu'ile de Quiberon (literally 'almost the island of Quiberon'). Early on the journey is bordered on each side by the sea; at one point, in bad weather the seas may actually unite. Quiberon town, at the southernmost point, is sheltered and, as well as being a busy harbour has an excellent sandy beach. From here one can board a ferry for the short crossing to Bell-Ile, once the summer retreat of Sarah Bernhardt. But, for a real contrast, return along the west coast of the peninsula. The dramatic grandeur of the Cote Sauvage should not be missed. Part way along is Camping Municipal du Kerne, a large well laid-out site with adequate facilities and moderately priced. Skirt the lake and cross the road and you are at the rock's edge. Take care here, rough seas can be dangerous.

We decided to take a giant leap along the coast to Port Louis. Along the way turn off to the Romanesque chapel of St. Cado, built by the Knights Templar in the 12th century. On a small island in the Etel estuary, it bears the name of a Welsh saint, around who is woven a tale of collusion with the Devil. As in all the best stories, the good guy comes out on top, and he got his causeway built. Use it to cross over and view the simple but impressive chapel and its adjacent Calvary.

Once known as Blavet (the river which guards it), Port Louis was re-christened in 1618 in honour of Louis XIII. Its granite-walled 17th century citadel watches over the gateway to its bigger brother L'Orient on the opposite bank. If you walk atop the ramparts adjoining the beach beware of vertigo and large people. There is no guard-rail, and the drop gets bigger and the way narrower. We left L'Orient for another time and took the road to Hennebont which is, sadly for it and for tourists, too easily by-passed on the N165 trunk road. Park by the river and walk up into the town's historic centre, alas badly damaged during the last war. Passing the 15th century fortifications call in at the 16th century church in the main square. Its 200 ft. spire dominates the town, whilst inside modern stained-glass windows and a 17th century organ co-exist comfortably. And when you are ready to depart go no further than the camp-site 100 yards alongside the river. At 14 francs for we two it was exceptionally good value, and can be highly recommended as an overnight stop.

Next day we took things quietly. Wishing to camp that evening near Vannes, we spent most of the time at Auray, and the associated Port St. Gustan. The latter is a jewel at the head of the river, and it was to here that the ships carrying Benjamin Franklin (American delegate to France during the American War of Independence, and the inventor of the lightning conductor) were directed to shelter during a great storm. The house he is reputed to have stayed in is now a hotel/café. The small quayside is bordered by them, and by the usual tourist traps. The port is linked to the town of Auray by a stone bridge, and the road climbs steeply into the town. From its ramparts one has a panoramic view over the port and surrounding countryside, a view much favoured by artists.

Late afternoon saw us on the D101 towards Vannes, a few miles short of which we diverted to Arradon, and on to our selected site by the side of the Gulf. Here at L'Allee is all the room one could wish for, either in open field or amidst a cider-apple orchard. The sight of a full-grown motorhome negotiating the branches and the fallen apples must have been impressive indeed – a bull in a china shop. Once, settled, we made use of the very well-appointed and well-kept facilities, before taking our evening stroll down to the water's edge. As dusk fell there was an air of magical mystery in the lights across the bay and the silhouettes of myriad boats. A calming and a soothing spot after a day's sightseeing.

And so to Vannes, a city for shopping and for sightseeing, of bargains and of beauty. The cathedral in the town's Old Quarter was six centuries in the building and contains the tomb of its patron, St. Vincent. Those seeking a centre from where to tour cannot do better than centralise on Vannes; the area is so full of history and archaeology, yet with a large and bustling market attracting crowds from miles around. We spent a few hours seeing the city's sights before regretfully starting our homeward journey north.

Have you ever been the only ones on a campsite? I mean, the ONLY ones. By evening we had arrived at a lovely site some 50 miles north of La Trinite-Porhoet. Adjacent to a lake and jogging-track, the site also boasts a well-equipped toilet block and a swimming pool. Being now at the end of August, it was out of the French camping season. However, at about 7pm the concierge appeared, alerted in her village home to our presence. We paid the nominal 14 francs asked. She switched on the electricity and hot water, and we were officially in – the only campers on the site. Autumn leaves floated on the pool's surface, and by 10 pm it was pitch dark.

Our holiday was nearly over, but one more night brought us one more excellent site in a beautiful location. On the way we visited Jugan-les-Lacs, a haven for sailors and surfers, and then on to Lancieux. The municipal site at the water's edge is just a short walk from the beach, and possesses excellent facilities. Lancieux has very good swimming, plenty of sand and boats, and many interesting architectural building styles.

Finally, on the morning of our last day on French soil we arrived at Dinard, and found parking to be a problem, especially if you want it free. Being larger than average, our motorhome was parked adjacent to the outdoor sea-water pool. If you try there, you need 2-franc pieces to load the meter, so be prepared. We required quite a few, as we had planned to walk the very picturesque headland pathway, to be followed by lunch at the Café Anglais. Naturally very popular with British tourists, it provides good local cuisine at affordable prices. And, oh yes, the local cider is served, chilled, in cups…the proper way to drink it, they say.

It was with regret that we prepared to depart French shores from the port of St. Malo. The evening sunshine turned to drizzle, and the rebuilt city walls became grey and grim. St. Malo had been almost totally destroyed during the last war, but had been faithfully rebuilt, and is well worth exploring. The outer walls provide an excellent platform from which to view the sea and the docks, and provides peeps into the city streets. So down into the maze of small cobbled street, and one immediately integrates with the mediaeval surroundings. We stayed a few hours only, but promised ourselves a return visit one day, both to St. Malo and to that lovely part of France which is the land of the Breton.

The Welsh Borders – The Marches

1995

The counties of Herefordshire and Shropshire boast many lovely little villages, and a wealth of history and related sites to read about and visit. The main centres of these counties are joined together by the A49, an umbilical cord of somewhat doubtful efficiency stretching from Shrewsbury to Hereford and beyond. This road, upgraded in places but in general falling woefully short of meeting the demands of today's traffic, passes through or alongside some of the loveliest countryside in England, much of it unspoilt either by overdevelopment or by tourism. The two counties have much in common; indeed, if Herefordshire had to be combined with another county, Shropshire would have been a more ideal choice, rather than Worcestershire. For our week in the area, we decided to opt for a central base and to travel out and about, so chose the Caravan Club site in the charming village of Leintwardine.

Leintwardine, as seen from the bridge on the South side

Despite a tricky entrance off the A4114, the site is clean though fairly basic, and has a friendly owner who was only too willing to discuss and advise on routes of exploration. From the south, the road enters the village over the river Teme - 200 yards westwards the river Clun has joined forces - which bubbles over a small weir and on eastwards to Ludlow.

The bridge at Leintwardine

On our left is the famous 'Lion at Leintewardine' Hotel, opposite which lies the village green. Across from here is the 'Fiddlers Elbow' chip shop behind which in season a small teashop is half-hidden, patronised by walkers and cyclists. Daily provisions can be purchased from either the petrol station shop or the butchers in the High Street, or at the small general store in Watling Street. This latter is indeed a stretch of the great Roman road stretching from Dover to Caerwent in South Wales. Between the two streets lies the Roman 'vallum' or rampart, one of the largest in Europe. Here stands the 13th century church of St. Mary Magdalene, inside which is to be found an impressive memorial to Sir Banastre Tarleton, who once fought alongside Cornwallis in the American War of Independance, and retired to the village in 1814, where he died aged 78 in 1833.

The Saxon village of Leintwardine was, unusually, built over the remains of the Roman town and military station of Bravonium, established here to control the Celtic hordes in the west. Even after the Romans had departed, the Welsh continued to give trouble and eventually Offa, king of Mercia, built his dyke along the then border to keep them at bay. The coming of the Normans in 1066 was followed in time by the erection of thirty-two castles along the border (or March) and their knights were the Marcher Lords, of which the most powerful were the Mortimers of nearby Wigmore. An era of uneasy peace was shattered once more by the Civil War and in 1649 the castles at nearby Brampton Bryan and Hopton played their part, culminating with the defeat of Owain Glendwr at the battle of Mortimer's Cross outside Kingsland.

Ludlow Corn Exchange

An essential excursion is to Ludlow, a pretty but hilly market town some eight miles to the east, now blessedly bypassed by the A49. Parking is easy to find, and that around the market place is adjacent to the town's ruined castle. Begun by another Norman Marcher lord, Roger de Lacy, as a stronghold to subdue the Welsh, it progressed to a fortified palace under the Mortimers. Since then, the castle has been home to Richard, Duke of York (Wars of the Roses), to the princes Edward and Richard (better known as the Princes in the Tower), and to Prince Arthur (son of Henry 7th) and his bride Catherine of Aragon. It was here that Arthur died of a fever after only a few months of marriage, and Catherine became the first wife of Arthur's brother, Henry VIII. After 1689 the castle was abandoned and is now an extensive ruin in the ownership of the Powis Castle estate. Entry charges are very reasonable, and during the annual Ludlow Festival each July Shakespearean productions are held here.

The town of Ludlow was laid out by the Normans in grid pattern, and its five major streets contain architectural styles spanning several centuries. Since the mid-sixteenth century, when it was for over one hundred years the virtual capital of Wales, Ludlow's importance as a political, cultural and trading centre grew rapidly, and the new wealth of its merchants led to the construction of many fine buildings, Of chief note are the timbered Feathers Hotel (originally a gentleman's residence and then home to the Court of the Marches), the Bull Ring and Tolsey, the Butter Market, Dinham House (where the brother of the Emperor Napoleon once stayed) and of course the parish church of St. Lawrence, dating from the 13th century. Walking down Broad Street we passed beneath the medieval gatehouse (the only such one remaining in the town), and out to the 14th century Ludford Bridge. From here the road climbs the Whitecliffe, from where can be gained the finest view of castle and town together.

Being right on the border, a visit to neighbouring Wales was called for. Some eight miles to the west is the small market town of Knighton, built on a steep hill right on Offa's Dyke, and typically Welsh. On the way we had passed a turn to Bucknell village, outside which is Coxall Knoll. Here, Caractacus (Caradoc) had made his last stand against the Roman invader, was taken prisoner and sent to Rome. In Knighton, grey stone abounds, as do Welsh accents, but the people nowadays are friendly and the coffee shop in the ironmongers is good for snacks. The Victorian clock presides over the square, facing the blue-and-white facades of the many shops owned by the Price family, whilst at the bottom of the hill is Harry Tuffin's supermarket, where the 'pile them high, sell them cheap' policy is evident. Just behind is the town's cattle market, though in today's BSE-affected environment we did not see any evidence of recent activity there.

Clun Castle

 Away north, through the quaintly-named village of New Invention, and eventually a rushing descent to the border town of Clun. Just prior to the narrow packhorse bridge we turned left and parked in the area on the right. here are toilets, a picnic area and explanatory notices relating to the ruined castle across the footbridge. Now in the care of English Heritage,(no entry charge), it was once home to the mighty border barons. During the Civil War the castle was finally slighted (blown up) by Parliamentarian forces and today only the great stone keep bears silent witness to a feudal way of life. In the town is the Buffalo Inn, its name recalling an abortive attempt last century to introduce that American beast into English pastures at Clun. It was here too that Sir Walter Scott stayed whilst writing his novel 'The Betrothed'. The window of the dining room looks across to the old Town Hall, now the Museum, where is housed a fascinating collection of artifacts reflecting life in bygone days. Amongst these are clogs, clay pipes from Pipe Aston (near Wigmore), and Clun chairs, for which the town was once justly famous, selling to the well-off burghers of Ludlow on market days. On our return to Leintwardine we diverted to the tiny hamlet of Hopton Castle. Built by Henry II, the castle ruins are not at present accessible to the public, but it was here that, in 1641, the most brutal massacre of the Civil War took place. Beseiged by Royalist troops from Ludlow, the Parliamentarian garrison eventually surrendered but almost all the defenders were murdered in cold blood in revenge for the trouble and casualties they had caused. A barbarous episode even for those days, when life was cheap.

Next day dawned crisp and bright, ideal walking weather, so we set off to visit Wigmore Castle, once the stronghold of the Mortimer family who, as Earls of March, held sway in the area through the 12th and 13th centuries. However, English Heritage is restoring the castle, and meanwhile it is closed to the public. As a border castle it was often in action against the Welsh, but its history is also closely connected with the English throne. It was a Mortimer who had the dubious honour of being the first person to be executed at Tyburn for his part in rebellion, and in the Wars of the Roses it was Edward Plantagenet, Lord of the Manor at Wigmore Castle in 1461 who then became Edward IV of England. Travelling south we came to Mortimer's Cross, today a few buildings grouped about the crossroads but on 3rd February 1461 was the site of the Battle of Mortimer's Cross, the decisive battle of the Wars of the Roses. East of the A4110 is the Great West Field where, after a murderous battle leaving four thousand dead, the nineteen-year old Edward proved the victor and became king of England. A mile further south, outside the Monument Inn by Kingsland, can be read the full details of that terrible day.

Kingsland is a pretty little village, its main street a pleasing mixture of black-and-white houses interspersed with Georgian facades. Its chief claim to notoriety is that Owen Tudor, fleeing from the battlefield after the defeat of the Lancastrians, took refuge in Angel House, from where, on betrayal, he was dragged, sent to Hereford and next day was summarily executed. We drove on to Yarpole, where a stream runs through the village centre, and several attractive timbered buildings - including a medieval gatehouse now known as the Bakehouse - are evident. The church has an impressive detached belltower but, it being lunchtime, we moved on to the Bell Inn, rightly famed for its culinary hospitality. After lunch we felt ready for that walk; across the B4362 is Croft Castle, a fortified manor house privately owned by the Croft family but now under the auspices of the National Trust. At the top of the drive we parked the car, donned our boots, and set off uphill past the castle's impressive curtain wall into the Forestry Commission plantation. A gate led through onto the ramparts of Croft Ambrey, an Iron-Age hill fort, from which superb views can be had in all directions. For the more intrepid, an alternative route back leads down through Fishpool Valley. Once past the ruined buildings deep in the woodland a track to the right angles up and emerges into parkland just north of the castle. Altogether, a pleasant and leisurely walk through beautiful countryside.

To close the day, we drove via Wigmore to just before Adforton, slipping off to the right along a lane to Wigmore Abbey. It was here that the Augustinian monks, after several false starts, finally built their abbey on land granted them by the Mortimer family, many of whom now lie there peacefully.

One of such starts had been at Shobdon, a few miles west, in the 12th century, building adjacent to a Norman church. This was eventually demolished in 1756 so that its owner could erect the present gothic fantasy Only the chancel arch and two doorways remain, re-erected further up the hill where today, known as the Shobden Arches, they look suitably dramatic. However, back at Wigmore, its Abbot was deposed at the dissolution of the monasteries by Henry VIII. Today, its ruins are integrated into Grange Farm. The road back to Leintwardine lies via Peytoe Lane, emerging just north of the campsite.

Should you not wish to self-cater in the evenings, meals can be obtained at the Lion Hotel, or at certain of the larger local hostelries. - the Baron of Beef at Bucknell, the Compasses at Wigmore, the Riverside Inn at Aymestry, or even Chinese cooking at the Monument, outside Kingsland. Within living memory, Leintwardine boasted four inns and two hotels. Today the Coopers Hotel and the Swan Inn are private homes, and the whereabouts of the Anglers Retreat has been mislaid. However, the Sun Inn in Rosemary Lane - a private house with a licence - is one of only six similar in the country, and entry is by invitation only. Latch onto a local in the know, and you're in. Otherwise, it's up through the village on the Ludlow road past Leintwardine Manor, once a gentleman's residence, then a boys' boarding school, a guest house, and now converted into apartments. A short distance on lies the Cottagers Comfort, (now the Jolly Frog) where we enjoyed a drink or two and excellent meals with George and Sally.

Spend a day, as we did, in South Shropshire. From our village we drove first to Craven Arms. Once a busy market centre, its busiest point today is another Harry Tuffins supermarket. Both the A49 and the railway to Shrewsbury pass through, and we likewise hurried on towards Church Stretton. Here, the middle of three Strettons in the valley between the Long Mynd and Wenlock Edge, can be found shops of all kinds, and to suit all tastes, especially if you have an interest in antiques and bric-a-brac. The indoor antiques market covers a large area on three floors, and houses a vast array of such items. It's a great fun place for browsing, anyway. Moving on, we took the road to Carding Mill Valley, where one can have a very pleasant outing (many coachloads do) but we branched left up Burway Hill, a narrow and twisty road not really suited to Motorhomes, but negotiable and leading to the top of the Long Mynd, and overlooking the Mill. Soon we came to the Portway, a prehistoric trading route where we were some 1700 feet above sea level, with a magnificent all-round view - to the west the Stiperstones, and eastwards the scarp of Wenlock Edge. We ran south-west along the Portway and soon the gliding Club came into sight. This side of the Mynd is so precipitous that the updraft makes it the ideal place for this sport. One can drive downhill past it to Asterton, but in our motorhome we decided that discretion etc, so retraced our steps and parked for a picnic. This attracted the inevitable sheep, at times in number. Do not feed, or others will receive the message and come charging over for their share. They are not easily dissuaded.

Stokesay Manor gatehouse

Back south and on the A49 we passed Acton Scott, which houses an interesting and well-visited farm museum. Just past Craven Arms is the entrance to Stokesay Castle. Built around 1240 as a manor house, its ambitious owner in 1291 added crenellations, since when it has assumed the title of 'castle'. It is approached over a small bridge across the encircling moat, then beneath an impressive Jacobean gatehouse and thence into the forecourt. During the Civil War its owner Lord Craven supported Charles 1st and in 1645 Cromwell's Roundheads besieged it. Fortunately, it surrendered almost immediately, so avoiding the destruction usually meted out. The castle is now in the care of English Heritage and well worth a visit. A personal stereo guided tour brings to life the sights and sounds of earlier times, and is free of charge.

One cannot surely leave this part of the Marches without visiting the famous Black-and-White villages. There is a handy leaflet which describes the Trail so that one gets the most out of the journey, and an article in MMM recently (February '97) dealt with this area. In Eardisland, do not miss the 17th century dovecote by the millstream, with its some 800 nesting alcoves, or the 13th century church with its timbered nave. In a corner of the churchyard is a moated mound on which once stood a wooden castle, guarding the river crossing in the troubled Border region. Nearby is Burton Court, housing a range of collections - costume, oriental dress, natural history and fairground models. In season visitors can PYO, and enjoy excellent cream teas. Move on to Pembridge, with parking and refreshments in the Heritage centre. The church of St. Mary is notable in that its belltower is completely detached from the main building, and is a pagoda-type structure wirh a close resemblance to the stave churches of Norway, Viking influence perhaps? South of the village is Dunkerton's Cider Mill, with shop, bar and restaurant and, of course, the traditional viewing of the mill and tastes of various ciders. Dilwyn is the archetypal village scene - cottages, shops and pub grouped about a small green, with chestnut tree and nearby church. Fortunately bypassed, the village has an atmosphere of peace and serenity. Further down the A44 is the best-known of the villages, Weobley. Once indeed a small town, it sent two Members of Parliament to Westminster, but has since declined greatly in importance. One result of the Reform Bill of 1832,which stopped the practice of Rotten Boroughs, was the destruction by the Lord of the Manor of 84 houses which he owned in the village, and no longer required for the housing of voters shipped in from elsewhere to ensure his election majority.

Next day, to restock the larder, we visited Leominster. Here,'Loyal to Leominster' signs were much in evidence, the local shopkeepers' answer to the new(ish) Safeway (now Morrisons) supermarket at Barons Cross on the town's western edge. It was here that local knights and barons had met in 1215 to discuss strategy before proceeding to Runnymede for their showdown with King John. Much of the town centre is medieval or Tudor in origin with narrow lanes, half-timbered houses and small shops much in evidence. Etnam Street, however, contains several examples of Georgian town houses. The town's two predominant buildings are the Priory Church, and the Grange in the adjacent park. This latter was originally erected at the top of Broad Street as the town hall, with the ground floor used as a market. It was moved in 1853 to its present site, and the ground floor built-in. Taking the old route of the A49 south we came to wooded Dinmore Hill, at the top of which is car parking, cafe and information centre for Queenswood Country Park. On over the top and down the steep incline and soon the right-hand turning to Dinmore Manor is sighted. The inventor of the reflecting lens - later used in the development of the 'cats eyes' on roads - lived here, and the Manor is still in the ownership of the Murray family. We found the music room of particular interest, as it houses a rare example of a self-playing Victorian Aoelian Pipe Organ. The collection of 1930's stained glass is also on view in the Cloisters, and certain other rooms in the house are also open to the public. Adjacent to the rock garden and its pools is the 14th century Commandery of the Knights Hospitaller of St.

John of Jerusalem which, alas, was closed when we visited. Our route back to camp took us north of Leominster along the A49. At Ashton we diverted to the Lower Hundred Craft Shop, once an old threshing barn, which now concentrates on pottery, wood-turning, enamels, resin animals and hand-painted candles. A quick partaking of refreshment, then across to the other side of the A49, and to Berrington Hall. Now a National Trust property, this 18th century mansion lies in an extensive park laid out by Capability Brown, and was originally built around 1780 for a former Lord Mayor of London. A restaurant and shop are on site.

The end of our week arrived all too soon and we reluctantly took leave of this section of the Marches. There is still much to see in the area, and more still if one drives out just a little further - the Cadfael connection at Shrewsbury, the historic town of Montgomery with its ruined 13th century castle, Richard's Castle, Bishop's Castle, the small border towns of Presteigne and Kington with its nearby Hergest Gardens, and of course Hereford itself. Other camping sites too are available, including the Arrow C & C Park at Eardisland, Green Pastures at Orleton, and the Engine & Tender PH at Broome. We treated our week as a 'taster', returning home convinced there are many good courses to follow, and we shall be back again to continue our explorations of this beautiful and unspoilt part of England.

BRIAN G. DAVIES

The Pilgrim Route to Compostela

1998

Having talked about it for some years, and taken heart from Club members encouraging us to "give it a go", we at last set out on our Motorhome journey of a lifetime. At first we thought that our 'van (a Swift Kon-Tiki 600 of 1989 vintage) - and perhaps ourselves too - were too old for such a trip, but eventually took out the relevant insurances, booked the ferry with the Motorhome Ticket Club, packed our Kontiki with winter clothing, food and reading matter, and set off in search of Dover. Being at the west end of the country we cover a fair few miles before La Manche ever hoves in sight.

As a holiday journey, that through France will be little different to those of many other club members. But how many of you have lost your 'van before even landing in France? By the time we discovered the correct deck, poor Connie was at the rear end, in splendid isolation and the return vehicles had already commenced loading. Still, once off we aimed at Abbeville where we were to visit the grave of Maureen's grandfather, killed in 1916 on the Somme. The cemetery is very well tended, with a Book of Remembrance including such personal details as are known on all buried there.

From here we visited Vendome and the nearby troglodyte caves at La Roque l'Eveque (some of these have now been adapted for mushroom growing, so dark are they), and passed by the castles of the Loire. We stayed two days on the very good-value municipal site at Montmorillon which, unusually, had a dryer as well as a washing machine, and on leaving visited the castle of Tours de Langest. This nowadays is a farmyard where we had to befriend the dog before being allowed to turn around and depart.

Troglodyte caves

After Perigueux, we diverted along the Dordogne valley to the hill village of Beynac, with its exceedingly steep streets, and then headed for our overnight stop at Fumel.

Hill village of Beynac

After two nights at Camping du Loup in Lourdes (near enough to town to be able to walk in and visit the Basilica) we set off for St Jean-Pied-de-Port, the acknowledged starting point on this route for crossing into Spain. Little did we know then of the club's experiences in the "puddles of Peterborough" - the floods there actually made headline news on French TV.

When driving in France there is much for us Brits to take notice of; they drive on the right (don't forget to do the same), petrol is cheaper, roads seem wider/longer, many roadside notices are not in our dictionary, and in April many campsites are closed or semi-functioning. Rarely if ever is one offered a discount... "if we had to reduce prices we wouldn't be open at all" seems to be the common refrain. But those that are open are usually above reproach, clean and well-maintained and with "chaud douches" included in the price. Our only gripe - those continental loos still exist in places.

Oh yes. Where were we going to? Well, in 1994 we came across a book dealing with "Walking the pilgrim route to Santiago", so we thought we'd track it (but in more comfort of course). The Camino runs from the French side of the Pyrenees to Pamplona, and then west to Santiago (named after Saint James the Apostle, brother of John). Pilgrims, cycling or walking, have first to negotiate that small hindrance... the Pyrenees. We, agreeably surprised by Connie's performance, sailed up and into the summit's snows, then down through the Roncevalles Pass to Pamplona, passing plodding pilgrims on the way. It's not done, we understood, to offer them a lift; defeats the object of their attempt.

Once in Spain the weather dried but became very cold. Our campsite there at Navarette (with its fantastic marble toilet blocks) saw blue skies and distant snowy mountains - and hundreds of Spanish campers. It was Good Friday and they were well and truly in residence. Each pitch consisted of caravan, awning, kitchen tent (fully plumbed in and with electric) and car parking space. Just like home - some even have gardens, and they chatter till two in the morning. Still, it was their holiday; we were just passing through, which we did the next day.

Pass over the Pyrenees

Camino de Santiago

Have you noticed how, on approaching Spanish cities, the nearer you get the less you see of the older parts? Instead, they are now surrounded by new high-rise apartments, five or six blocks deep, like massive guardians, and very intimidating. Once through though, it's worth the effort to see Logrono, Burgos and Leon, with graceful tree-lined avenues and steeped in history. However, after going down a one-way street in the wrong direction and having to make a 3-point turn (how did I do that... desperation!) we tried to stick to smaller places. Like Carrion - find the site if you can; like L'Hospital Orbiga, once a pilgrim hospital on the Camino, and with a magnificent 20-arched cobbled bridge; like Sahagun, with its ancient monastery and massive town gateway, and Pontferrada, with its huge storks hovering over their nests on the castle, like prehistoric birds of prey.

Arco de San Benito, Sahagun

Near to Castlejeriz we met and talked with a group of young French pilgrims from Montpelier, displaying the pilgrim emblem of a cockleshell, and carrying and reciting from religious texts. By having their passports stamped at intervals along the way, they are entitled to free overnight stays at refugious, and by day walk between 25-35 kilometres. The trek from St. Pied-de-Porte takes them about two weeks to cover the 400 odd miles to Santiago.

Our own experience of that city was depressing. Truly, to travel was proving for us better than to arrive. Firstly, we couldn't find the campsite (the Michelin Guide said near the Airport) so eventually we wild-camped on a spur overlooking the city. Up early next morning in pouring rain, we found that the site was signposted 100 yards further on, near to another sign displaying "No wild camping in the city". Tough, though technically we hadn't. It was too wet to park and walk any distance to the Cathedral so we innocently drove into the old city, waved "hello/goodbye" to the resting place of Saint James, and sought for our exit. Narrow street, tight corners, morning rush hour.... and still raining stair rods. Were we glad to get out again. Found a bank for changing travellers cheques, so parked on a bus stop and dashed in. Twenty minutes later and mucho yappo with head office and "Sorry, we can't change Thomas Cook travellers cheques." Must be a first. So we gladly shook the rain from our tyres and headed north towards the Galician capital of La Coruna, once home to the Spanish Armada. This old city of Roman origin is today a busy international port, and is renowned for its miradores (glazed galleries on houses fronting the main street), the lighthouse Tower of Hercules, and the castle/fortress of San Anton.

The north coast of Spain is known as the "Green coast" and we soon discovered why. In general if it wasn't raining, it just had been. To add to this, campsites in that north-western corner are few, with even fewer open out of season. Another bash at wild-camping, this time outside a closed campsite (Spanish law permits this). We stuck to the coast road and were rewarded by majestic scenery of cliffs, beaches, tree-covered slopes and, of course, tortuous winding though well-surfaced roads. It was in this area that we noticed many men with umbrellas, cows with coats on, and those most indigenous of Asturian sights - the borreos, or grain barns. The small port of Riberdero nearly saw an end to our journey. It being market day, we decided to exit via a minor road towards the harbour. Passing two amazed Guardia on the narrow descent, we were unable to negotiate in one a tight turn near the bottom. I stopped and selected reverse... nothing doing. She just wouldn't go in, and the more I panicked the worse things got, edging us nearer and nearer to the wall, and the drop beyond. It was only after some four or five minutes of sweat and prayers (and some unrepeatables, no doubt), with a bemused but fortunately patient Spaniard behind me, that she eventually slotted in, and we were able to continue our descent. Another inch, and it would have required a tow from behind to extricate us.

After all this, it was a relief to leave the coast and head up the very impressive gorge towards Potes in the Picos de Europa. Extra care is needed here but the result is rewarding. The small mountain town is surrounded by snowy peaks, and we can recommend the campsite of La Viorna (again boasting a washing machine and a dryer). We stayed two nights, taking the opportunity in incessant rain to shop and dine in the town. The next day in brilliant sunshine we ventured to the road's end at Funte De, where snow was abundant, and from where a funicular ascends to a nearby peak. A snowplough had recently been in action, and the roads here were clear. Back on the coast, we made for Guernica (site of the infamous Fascist air attack of the Spanish Civil War) and round past Bilbao and San Sebastian, from where a new motorway crosses the mountains and down to Pamplona. We found the Spanish roads fascinating. Well-surfaced, often new or newly aligned, across viaducts and through several tunnels (and with petrol - and wine - even cheaper than in France); EEC money has certainly been spent to the benefit of the local economy and tourist traffic alike. But have a care; where roads are dug up, both sides are involved and long stretches of gravel, dust or mud may have to be negotiated in both directions. Still, perhaps the job gets done quicker - or more cheaply - this way, but it isn't good for a motorhome's suspension. The road (N260) between Sabinanigo and Pont de Suert, our next evening's stop, is as varied a scenario as it is possible to get.

Deserted village in the Pyrenees

Imagine a steep ascent followed by a tunnel to the Puerto de Cotefablo; a long descent to the plain, where we came across several deserted and ruined villages, through a moonlike landscape of weather-carved strata and hilltop villages; and a very narrow and winding gorge dropping down again to a friendly and well-equipped site at Alta Ribagorga (the owner runs a bar across the road) a few miles before the town. Enquiring there about the deserted villages, which we had put down to pestilence or to brigand activity, we were told it was nothing more exciting than the old dying off, the young moving off, and the markets for their produce dropping off. Seemed a terrible waste of resources.

We were stopped, twice by custom officials. Faced with "have you got any cigarettes, alcohol or drugs?" what would you say? So, NO to ciggies and drugs - no mention of the gallons of drinkies out of sight under the seats. After a quick passport check we were allowed to proceed; I wonder why they don't ask these questions of you at the border any more, but sneak them at you on the open road. Though after France, Spain and Andorra what do you expect? And anyway, I'm a compulsive shopper in foreign supermercados, much to Maureen's apprehension, and bottles appear in the trolley all the time. At Pas de la Casa we were even given a bottle of wine for being such good customers. We exited Andorra via the Col de Puymorens, leaving the last of the snows to the skiers, and dropped into France for the run up to Perpignan. This valley is notable for its fortress villages of Mount Louis and Villefranche, and for the "little yellow train" which clings to cliff faces and spans gorges on impressive viaducts... a fabulous piece of engineering. Later on we became embroiled in a local version of the "Tour de France".

The Cathdral at Elne

Everything gets out of the way of these cyclists, and the towns and villages along the way are lined with cheering crowds. What a welcome, we thought, until the support car let us have their horns full blast. That told us! Now in Catalonia (French side) we diverted briefly to visit the cathedral at Elne, Vauban's immense fortress at Collioure, and the rugged coastline around Banyuls-s-Mer and Cerbère, hard by the Spanish border.

Cap Cerbère Lighthouse

Then north again via Argeles, the great salt lake at Bacarès, and the historic cities of Narbonne and Beziers. Near to this latter we had our first trouble; trying to reverse in a small village square I sideswiped a tree (swear it just jumped out at me). The front bumper cover became dislodged but fortunately looked worse than it was. Staying with friends soon after for a short break we had it repositioned.

Staying with friends, with their dog

Then, once again well and truly in the mountains pushed on past Puy to the walled town of Langeac. Here, the campsite adjoined the river, and contained dire warnings of flooding, with diagrams of how to escape should the waters rise. Fortunately, that night they didn't, and next day we took advantage for a while of the quite pleasant (and free) A75 towards Clermont-Ferrand. Again, we were unimpressed by a large, busy and advert-cluttered approach so we pressed on via Vichy and Nevers, both well worth a visit. That evening we descended towards the then (to us) little-known city of Auxerre, with its well-equipped campsite opposite the football stadium (how the World Cup has educated us since).

Our final day in France - a Sunday - and the contact between the ignition and the starter motor broke down. A call to the French RAC eventually got us limping on to Calais, for a night on the dockside. By 8am next morning we were aboard and, some 400 miles later and considerable palaver to make contact manually every time we had to re-start were at last safely home. However, if those were the only problems in over 4500 miles of continental driving, we counted ourselves lucky.

Despite our initial fears, it had been a great trip, and a wonderful experience, and our thanks to those members of the club who encouraged us to get on with it. Had we not done so now, who knows... would we have done it in the future? After all, both I and Connie are getting on a bit. Now, though, we are all looking for new lands to visit, new sights to see, but we shall never forget the thrills of this journey and the many places we were able to touch upon. There is indeed, nothing like Motorcaravanning.

Singapore: The Lion City

1998

As a long-time Timeshare owner, I contacted Interval International to request a 2-week holiday in Singapore, using a week of Timeshare at Four Seasons, Marbella, and a second week at La Orquidea, Malaga, for any period in October.

I was immediately offered an exchange to the Amara Lifetime Hotel, which is II's only resort in the city, so I duly paid my exchange fees and confirmed our booking. The process was very easy and we were pleased to have got what we wanted, when we wanted it. All we had to do now was to look forward to this unique holiday.

The Amara Hotel

Our flight from Heathrow departed at midday in bright sunshine as we settled back in the luxury of our Economy

Class flight. Singapore Airlines operate Boeing Megatop B747-400s on this route and boast three classes of accommodation – First, Raffles and Economy. If this was the latter, what luxury could the others offer? Seating was comfortable, with ample space, our hostesses brightly garbed in traditional design, and a Krisworld entertainment centre for each passenger was designed to keep us interested, informed and amused. Over the next 12 hours we could follow our journey on the video monitor as we flew over Europe, the Middle East, India and Malaya, before touching down in the late afternoon, still relaxed, well-fed and in anticipatory mood, at Changi International Airport, Singapore – almost right on time.

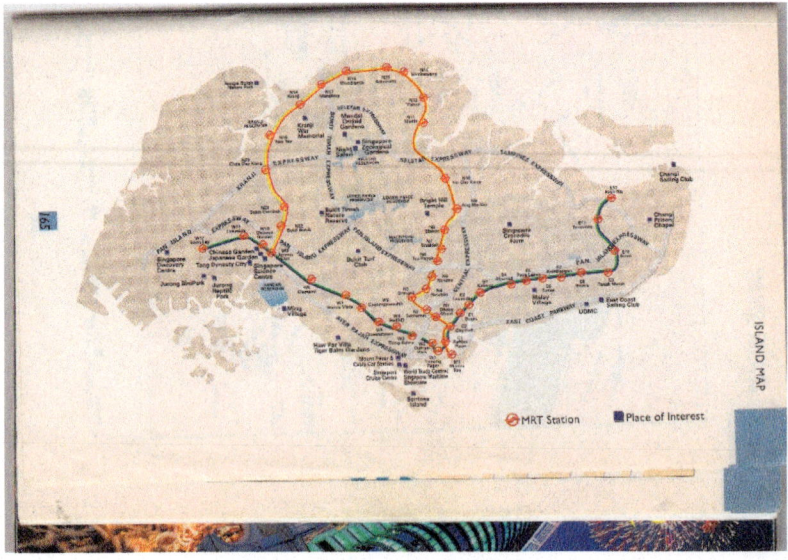

Map of Singapore's MRT service

Exiting the air-conditioned coolness of the airport we walked unsuspectingly into the 33-degree "Turkish Bath" heat of the island. We quickly found a taxi (also air-conditioned) and directed it to our destination in the Tanjong Pagar district of the city. We were extremely fortunate to be staying at the Amara Lifetime Hotel, right on the southern edge of the city's commercial centre. From here, whether by bus, MRT (Metro) or taxi, travel was easy and cheap and we soon abandoned our first thoughts of hiring a car – it just wasn't necessary. In any case, Singapore's road pricing policy aims to keep excessive traffic off their roads, and we went along with that.

A typical street scene

The Singaporeans delight in dining out; restaurants of all persuasions abound – Nonya (the local cuisine), Chinese, Indian, Malay, Indonesian, Japanese. Thai, even Italian, whilst Food Courts and Hawker centres are everywhere. In these we found more down-to-earth meals at very down-to-earth prices; twice we dined for $7.50 in total – two meals for £3, and very satisfying they were too. Exotic drinks were available everywhere; guava and soursop fruit drinks, coconut milk (direct out of the husk) and sugarcane, chrysanthemum teas and iced coffee (Starbuck's Coffee House, is noted for this) and the ubiquitous gin-based Singapore Sling in the Long Bar at Raffles Hotel (at £8 a time). Tiger beer is plentiful though pricey, whilst wine is both expensive and, in that humid climate, unnecessary.

A MTR and a new town

The Mass Rapid Transit (MRT) is the main form of transport in those areas where its ever-growing tentacles spread out to. It is highly efficient, safe and, fortunately, air-conditioned. We were most impressed by its platform safety doors, and by the palatial aspects of its underground stations within the city limits. It was in one of these that we saw the sign "No Durians Allowed". What were these, some breed of gypsy, perhaps? No, they are a very smelly local fruit, the aroma from which hangs about for a long time, and is most difficult to remove. They are banned in hotel foyers too. The MRT has two lines, one from west to east and the other looping north to the Causeway connecting Singapore to mainland Malaya, returning by a different route. A third line is under construction, north-east from the World Trade Centre to a hitherto under-developed area. We took a round trip on the northern loop (actually incurring a $2 fine for overstaying the permitted 75 minutes of travel (how were we to know about that?) but it was worth it and we soon got a good idea of suburbia and the ongoing development of the island.

Having been stationed in Singapore for my National Service in the 50's my recollections of the hinterland were of almost complete jungle and dirt roads, save for those areas of armed forces occupation. Today, virgin jungle has largely given way to concrete jungle. Huge New Town conurbations along the routs of the MRT, their Housing Development Board blocks (some 60% of the population currently live in these) crowding closely together and – like the office skyline of the city itself- reaching ever higher into the skies. Parkways and expressways criss-cross the island, aiding the ever-continuing development of suburbia, where many unfinished buildings are swathed in colourful green or blue safety netting. And, seemingly, people are ever available to occupy both HDB and private accommodation; an island about the size of the Isle of Wight now supports a population approaching 5 million, and still growing.

Riding the MRT

Our hotel accommodation consisted of two large rooms, one with an "Emperor-sized bed, a mini-fridge, a safe, coffee-making facilities, TV and air-conditioning and with ample room to spread. When I stated that one room would be sufficient for us we were informed "You have exchanged two rooms, so here you get two rooms", including two fridges and two bathrooms…all very civilized. We were at all times treated as full-paying guests and all the hotel services (maid, room cleaning, and complimentary newspaper – the Straits Times) and facilities (open-air rooftop pool, laundry, money-changing and its five restaurants) were freely available to us. The hotel also had a gift shop, and was linked direct into an adjacent shopping mall and Food Court – all so very convenient. Timeshare remained discreetly in the background, but the arrangements made by Interval International for our comfort were excellent. However, we were in Singapore on holiday, so most of the time was spent away from base.

Saint Andrew's Cathedral

We must have walked miles about the city, visiting Raffles Hotel, Raffles City (a huge new shopping complex), Clark Quay and Boat Quay (a must for the evening 'stroll and dine'), Suntec City and Marina Square (more shopping), and the old Colonial District with its Victoria Theatre, Parliament House and City Hall. We took the MRT to Orchard Road – their equivalent of London's Oxford Street and the location of many of the international hotels. We visited St. Andrew's Cathedral by the Padang – an island of peace 'midst the surrounding bustle, joined in a Sunday morning Chinese Methodist English service where we were warmly greeted by the congregation, and tentatively entered Hindu temples and Buddhist centres of worship. We also shopped in Chinatown (a silk Kimono for £12), Arab Street and Little India where, on the eve of Duvali, we mingled with over ten thousand celebrating Indians. Singapore is proud of its multi-racial society, and we enjoyed soaking up its ethnic atmosphere.

A Buddhist temple

Away from the city we went to Haw Par Villa (the old Tiger Balm Gardens Chinese theme park), to Tang Dynasty City which depicts an impressive period of Chinese history, and the Malay Village, the Boating Gardens and the Chinese Gardens with its pagodas, temples and teahouse.

Haw Par Villa entrance

We called at my old army location at Ulu Pandan (now a depot of the S.A.F. Military Police, and visited the Battle Box at Fort Canning, once the HQ of SEAC, and experienced the animatronics and video presentations of events leading up to the surrender of the British Forces in 1942 to the invading Japanese. From Clifford Pier we took a Chinese "junk" cruise through the busiest harbour in the world in a replica of Cheng Ho, a Chinese Imperial vessel of the Ming Dynasty, landing for a short time on Kusu to see its temples and its many turtles.

The Cheng-Ho vessel

A whole day was spent on Sentosa Island, previously known as Blakang Mati (and where I had once been stationed for a few days on an army instructional course), and the location of three forts constructed for the abortive defence of Singapore. It is now a pleasure island for Singaporeans and tourists alike. We crossed over by cable car 180ft above the docks, from its station on Mount Faber, and made good use of the free monorail to explore the island.

The aerial way to Sentosa

We visited the Singapore Experience -a museum depicting both the history of Singapore and the local ethnic customs and festivals. We walked around Fort Silosa and into the labyrinth of tunnels. We took the lift to the top of the Merlion (the symbol of Singapore since 1972), a huge hollow structure some 37 metres high. From here we could see back to the city skyline of towering office blocks and hotels, nearer to Keppel Wharf and the Tanjong Pagar with their myriad of container traffic, and out to sea to the oil-depot isle of Paulo Bukum. We did not have time to visit the Asian Village, the Butterfly Farm, Underwaterworld or Volcanoland, nor to make use of the swimming lagoons. A spectacular display of dancing fountains closed our evening, with lasers beaming from the eyes of the Merlion.

On Sentosa with the Merlion

Singapore's International airport is at Changi, to where the MRT will not reach until 2002. It is largely constructed on land reclaimed from the sea but once was the site of the notorious prisoner-of-war camp in which the Japanese interned military and civilian personnel alike. Nearby is Changi's prison chapel, open by appointment and a stark reminder of those grim days. Since my days Singapore Island has expanded considerably through reclamation, no area more so than on its south-eastern edge where today the East Coast Park now lies – a rest and recuperation area for residents – and along which runs the East Coast Parkway, joining the city to its airport.

Our time to depart came all too quickly. We'd had no time to visit other places of interest – the Jurong Bird and Parrot centre, the Crocodile Centre, the Ming Village, the Zoological gardens, the Discovery Centre or the Bukit Timah Nature Reserve (at the summit of which I had spent many visits in 1953 with soldiers from my unit, introducing them to the mysteries of map-reading). Meanwhile, a taxi conveyed us from our hotel to the airport's terminal 2, where we were to board our return aircraft. We had quickly adapted to the foreign faces around us, principally Chinese (80%), with a smattering of Indians (7%) and Malays and other races. English is the 'lingua franca' connecting us all and we had no problem at all communicating. Newspapers and TV are freely available in English (or at least American). We had been impressed by Singapore's cleanliness, its freshness (even in a 33 degree heat), the neatness of dress of its inhabitants (schoolchildren all wear school uniform which contributes much to this impression), and with the overall feelings of well-being safety ever-present. At no time did we feel threatened, drunks and beggars were hardly ever seen and – due perhaps to the strictness of its ant-crime laws or perhaps the high incidence of its inhabitants who carry mobile phones with them everywhere, including and especially children as they travelled the MRT - we came across no instances of lawbreaking. During our time in Singapore we met tourists from all-over who were either just passing through or on multi-location trips around south-east Asia, and who could at best only touch upon the sights and delights of this island city-state. Singapore's holiday potential is, we feel, much under-rated by Europeans. We were glad to have opted to spend our whole time here, not even being tempted to dilute the experience by crossing the causeway into Johore. We had spent two weeks here, but another few weeks would have been needed for a more comprehensive visit, and that we regret we do not have……..at least, not yet.

Dream On In Canada

1999

We saw it advertised on the back of a magazine - Good Times, "Holidays to exciting places", it said. The Grand Canyon, New England, Alaska, the Rockies... stop right there. And by motorhome too. As long-time motorhome owners we were attracted by the propsect of a 2-week drive through the Canadian Rockies, from Calgary to Vancouver. So in August 1998 we sent off to Escorted Motorhomes in Surrey for their brochure, and spent many subsequent hours mulling over the information, looking at pictures, and doing our costings. The brochure said... "Dream on..." and we did, eventually deciding to say "Yes". We sent our deposit, and then spent more time thinking up queries, which were helpfully and courteously answered by Philip Marshall of E.M. Twelve months passed, during which flights were books, excursion options chosen, insurance and driving details checked, and additional hotel nights in Vancouver confirmed... all done very efficiently for us through and by E.M.

We flew from Heathrow at the end of July, and were met on landing at Calgary by one of the Wagonmasters who would be travelling with us, both to provide information and to take care of the unforeseen. We were taken to the Best Western Hotel near to the airport - prebooked and incuded in the holiday cost - for our first night's stay, and met the others in our group next morning. After a substantial breakfast we, with four other couples, were bussed to the nearby depot to pick up our motorhome. We had booked a 24-footer, with full-size fridge/freezer and (ah, luxury!) made-up bed, though there had been 28-foot beasts on offer too. Ours proved to be quite adequate for two, and easily manageable on the Canadian roads. After the initial introduction to the vehicles we all set off for Safeways to stock up for the journey ahead.

Collecting the R.V.

Our Arvee (RV) - as it designated over the pond - was automatic, had power steering and cruise control, and air conditioning. E.M. had provide a full tank of gas (sorry, propane) for cooking and running the fridge/freezer, and all crockery and linen were included in the pack. The vehicle had a new-to-me clutch system, with a steering column lever and, for a few panicky moments I had been left behind, wondering how to get the 'van moving. The CB radio came in handy at the start... "Put your foot on the handbrake before selecting drive". Once I'd got my head around that one we were off and so, gingerly at first, then with confidence growing, we made our way through the Calgary suburbs, with their myriad cross-roads and traffic lights, towards the open road and increasingly impressive scenery. 90 miles on was our first night's stay, in Banff National Park (it costs $8 per person to enter these parks), and it was early evening when we arrived at the Tunnel Mountain campsite above Banff township. This site holds over

1000 units, all well spread out amid stunning scenery, and parked on roadways...the grassy areas are for barbecues and picnics - and it was full. Fortunately E.M. do where possible prebook their pitches, and at this and others we stayed at later, such foresight paid off, as we were travelling at the height of the area's limited holiday season.

Tunnel Mountain campsite, Banff

That evening our Wagonmasters, Martin and Kenny, put on a super barbecue, at which we munched, drank, and chatted, or simply took in the majesty of the surroundings, with Mount Rundle overlooking the whole site, the evening rays glancing off its rocky outlines. The only downside - the mosquitoes, much bigger and fiercer than our own. Once out of the towns, mozzies are everywhere, with their painful bites to prove it. We soon learned that a good application of repellent (we were advised to get OFF) was a necessity, but at times they still chewed their way into us. Still, it was a small price to pay for the fabulous views and scenery we were - and would be - seeing as we travelled through this entrancing landscape.

Awaiting the helicopter

We had opted for the scenic helicopter flight-seeing, and next morning were led by one of our Wagonmasters to the heliport outside neighbouring Canmore. We had a 20-minute wait, spent in watching a video and gawping at the 'copters coming and going. Once strapped in and headphones donned, the helicopter lifted off smoothly, circling the neighbourhood before climbing rapidly towards the distant snow-covered peaks of Mount Assiniboine.

Mount Assiniboine

Being our first such flight, it was akin to ascending into heaven, with icefields below us, and rocky crags pushing through their ancient snows. The views were stupendous, and we were glad we had chosen this half-hour flight as our main option. Back at ground level and after a brief encounter with the gift shop, we set off to explore Canmore, before returning to our site for lunch.

City of Banff

The afternoon saw us catch the 'bus into Banff, overlooked by Cascade Mountain, and where in glorious sunshine we were able to shop and sightsee, and to send our first postcards home... not an easy thing as Banff does not allow postboxes on its streets; you have to go to the post office for that. The majority of the population appeared to be Japanese, and indeed many from that country were either rubber-necking by the coachload, or had emigrated to Banff and were now either working in or owning a large number of the tourist shops in that town. And all the time, RVs were passing and re-passing... there were even special parking areas allocated to them, and free at that. And with petrol at the equivalent of 25 pence per litre, what more could a tourist want? We did not have time to take in the gondola ride up Suphur Mountain, with its fabulous panoramas over the town, nor to visit the Banff Springs Hotel and the Hot Springs spa. Perhaps next time?

Next morning it was "wagons roll", down through Banff and across the Canadian Pacific railroad, where we saw the 'Rocky Mountaineer' standing at the station. We have that in mind for another year! Driving on the right didn't pose a problem, as we visit the European continent frequently, and I found the "Turn Right if safe to proceed" arrow at cross-roads very useful.

At the far end of Lake Louise

So on to the Trans Canada Highway and towards Lake Louise, surely one of the most beautiful and photogenic spots in the whole country. On the way we diverted onto Highway 1A, a less frequented route the other side of the Athabasca river valley, and on which we saw a number of road-skiers zooming along on a sponsored outing. After a brief stop at Castle Village (where we bought lovely pecan tarts) we continued on towards Lake Louise. The car park was crowded but we were fortunate to catch a large vehicle leaving so we gently eased into the vacant space, and made our way to the lakeside with the magnificent and world-famous hotel (Chateau Lake

Louise) situated at its head. Here we wandered through the foyer, and the many shops lining its colonnade. In the distance we could see the Victoria glacier, the sunshine striking off the ice like diamonds.

Victoria Glacier

The day was now hot so gently we walked to the far end of the lake, where again we encountered those curious little mammals, marmots (or ground squirrels) which had been plentiful also at Tunnel Mountain, and whose two-legged antics are a sight to behold. Later, we drove to Moraine Lake, famous for the huge pile of glacial rubbish at its entry, and for its remarkable turquoise colour caused by deposits of "rock flour". I was fascinated by its log-jam, and tried a spot of log-walking, but only got past two logs, and wet feet for my efforts. Not my thing, I felt. Two miles North of Lake Louise Village is the Summer Sightseeing Chairlift, which whisked us in an open ride to the upland mountain areas. During this 10-minute ride we saw our first bear... a big grizzly, fortunately quite a way below us, searchig for food in the bushy undergrowth.

Moraine Lake

At the top we looked back at distant Lake Louise, centrally nestling in its vast mountain range, snowy peaks all about, and felt very conscious of our insignificance. But evening was drawing on and we had to make landfall at Kicking Horse campground in the Yoho National Park, so we set off again towards the steep descent of the Great Divide, where waters flow either to the Atlantic or to the Pacific. Along the way we viewed the Spiral Tunnels which enable the railways to climb up the pass, and inn the early evening arrived at our destination, a wilderness site surrounded by more of those peaks we were by now becoming used to.

The campgrounds we were using varied both in standard and in the facilities provided. Some were top-level, and provided on-pitch access to water, electricity, waste water dumping, picnic table and on accasion even barbecue equipment with logs as requjired. At others, our pitches may not have any of these things, water provided by a central tap, and the only toilet facilities a "shack" with a pan suspended over a bottomless (no pun intended) pit. Still, our 'vans were self-sufficient, with fresh water, 12-volt electricity, propane, a bathroom with loo and shower, and waste-water dumping equipment. So it was no hardship to "self-cater" now and then.

We were up very early the following morning, and by 7am were having breakfast, facing the magnificent Takakkaw Falls, one of the highest in Canada. But our journey towards the Columbian Snowfield beckoned, as we had planned to arrive by lunchtime, but the very many scenic stops along the way disrupted our timetable considerably. Re-entering Banff National Park we headed north along the Icefields Parkway, one of the most scenic drives in North America. Now came spectacular waterfalls, beautiful lakes and over one hundred glaciers along the route.

Bow Lake

Cameras in hand, we captured the majesty of the peaks surrounding Crowfoot Glacier, and reflected in the still waters of Bow Lake, stopped off to view the aquamarine of Lake Peyto - the highest of the Parkway at almost 7000 feet - and paused briefly at the many breathtaking sights along the way. It was well past lunchtime before we pulled into the Columbia Icefield Centre, halfway along the Parkway. There was a half-hour queue to get our tickets for the trip onto the Athabasca glacier, but at last a bus took us to the starting point, where we transferred onto a Snowmobile - a weird-looking multi-coloured vehicle with huge wheels needed to provide the necessary grip on the ice. It was a fantastic experience, riding on 200-year old snow up to 300 metres deep, with the mountains and their hanging glacier and icefields all about. It was chilly on the glacier itself, the wind coming off banks of serrated hardpacked snows stretching ahead of us. We were told that at the end of the 19th century the glacier had been over a kilometre longer, reaching to the site of today's Centre buildings. Where would it be after the next hundred years, we wondered?

On the Athabasca Glacier

Soon after our departure we passed into Jasper National Park (another $8 each), and headed for our campground outside Jasper. There were still places to see - Tangle Falls, Sunwapta Falls, Athabasca Falls - where the road climbed steeply up a winding section of roadway - but at last we diverted before the town into Whistlers Campground, where we were to stay for two nights to allow us to explore the area. We had been allocated individual pitches, separated by bushes or trees, and although this site too was fully booked its layout helped keep down the noise level. That evening, it being our wedding anniversary, Maureen and I tried out one of the town's many restaurants, and found dining out to be quite reasonably priced. Next day, whilst some of the others - mad fools! - went white-water rafting, we drove into Jasper and parked alongside the railroad. RVs were everywhere, seeming to be at least one out of every three vehicles. We found the town to be a useful stopover, and made good use of its pretty Information Centre - built in 1913 - and the many tourist shops. Also displayed to effect is a Canadian Pacific steam locomotive and a magnificent totem pole. We also found a petrol station which provided a free waste-water dump for RVs. That's what we call service.

Our anniversary barbecue

On the second evening we were very surprised - and of course pleased - to be guests at a barbecue secretly arranged for us on site by E.M. and our fellow travellers. Kenny again came into his own as chef, and the fire blazed late into the night.

Jasper is surrounded by mountains and lakes in abundance. From the main street we could see Mount Edith Cavell, Pyramid Mountain and Whistlers Mountain, to the summit of which can be taken a Skytram ride for a bird's eye view over the town.

Lake Maligne

We drove to see Lake Maligne, passing Medicine Lake enroute. This latter is a strange lake of over 20 metres depth in summer, but disappears when winter comes, as the snows hold the feedwaters, and the lakewater runs off underground for many kilometres, to emerge at Maligne Canyon. We also drove several miles north of Jasper along Rte. 16 towards Edmonton, seeing elk grazing at the road's edge, goats scavenging along the highway, and stopped off to view the sulphur spring issuing from a small cleft in the roadside rock.

Robson Meadows Campground

Our next night was to be spent at Robson Meadows campground, opposite Mount Robson itself, the highest point in the Rockies at almost 13,000 feet. We drove here via the Yellowhead Highway, crossing the boundary between the Parks near the Overlander Falls. Once again we were on a wilderness site with few facilities. A short drive past the visitor centre - from where we had a glorious view of this magnificent peak - found us at a footbridge over the Robson River, bringing with its rumbling waters a stream of freezing air - a temperature we were not used to. Behind us we could see Mount Terry Fox, so named in 1981 to honour the cancer victim who had, during his attempt to run across Canada, raised $25million for cancer research.

Next morning we were off again down the Highway Route 5 to Valemont, where we stocked up before continuing on to Blue River junction. The highway parallels both the North Thompson River, and the Canadian National Railway, which took a route alternative to that chosen by Canadian Pacific in its race across the Rockies. At the visitor centre here, with its magnificent statue of a moose (the only time we ever saw one, as in summer they stay in the uplands) we turned into Wells Gray Provincial Park, located in the Caribou Mountains. Twenty miles along Clearwater Valley Road the road deteriorated into a 'graded gravel surface', all holes, bumps and ridges. For relief we diverted up an unmade road leading, several interesting miles later, to Green Mountain, where there were fabulous views from a lookout tower to the surrounding peaks. Back on the gravel road we were continually thrown around, and somewhere along the route lost our wastewater hose, which flew out of its compartment. Fortunately, Wagon Masters carry spares, and this was easily remedied.

It was along here too that we encountered our first black bear... he stepped out onto the roadway some 50 yards ahead, took a leisurely look at us as we crawled towards him, and ambled back into the undergrowth, having decided not to stop for a photo session.

Tour to Rainbow Falls

We were to stay at this campground for two nights, to allow us to take the optional boat tour along Clearwater and Azure Lakes to Rainbow Falls. Everyone had booked for this four-hour trip, and we watched fascinated as the helmsman avoided the many tree-trunks and other debris floating on or below the surface. On landing at a sandy beach, we were able to walk through the forest to the falls, examining on the way a cache... two trees with a high-level platform slung between them for food storage, the treetrunks encased partway up with a shiny metal to prevent bears climbing to get at the food. This is a very real danger where people may leave food accessible... and a fed bear is a dead bear, as the saying goes, as they get into the habit of approaching human habitation for their food. On our return we clearly saw an osprey and a bald eagle perched in the tree-tops... two more to tick off.

Our way out of the park led first past Helmcken Falls, which at 137 metres is higher than Niagara, and then Dawson Falls, both worth the small diversion. Back on the highway we had all day to reach that night's stopover outside Clinton, so at Little Fort we branched off and up on route 24, following the route to Green Lake, where we picnicked at a well-equipped lakeside beach, and then turned south on Route 97 to the Painted Chasm. This is a geological wonder 120 metres deep, the rocky sides of which seem to be painted in horizontal bands of various colours. Then on through Clinton, which is on the way to the Caribou goldfields, and which was once a popular stopover for weary prospectors. Lake View campground was not too far on from here, and we were at last on this site to take advantage of laundry facilities.

Next day our journey initially followed the Thompson River, which at Lytton joined the Fraser River. The combined waters widened and deepened, and at Hell's Gate, where we took the Airtram across the canyon, the river is unbelievably some 300 feet deep. The Visitor Centre here boasts a restaurant, a gift shop, and a fudge factory shop, with more varieties than we had ever dreamed of, and there is also a suspension bridge across the river. A salmon ladder has been constructed to enable the fish to bypass the huge amount of detritus in the river, and climb towards their spawning grounds. From this point on, two railroads run alongside the river, one each side of the canyon.

Airtram over Fraser River at Hell's Gate

At last the descent levelled off, and we by-passed the township of Hope, once the centre of the fur and goldrush trades, as we made our way along Route 1 towards Harrison Hot Springs and our overnight at Sasquatch Springs RV campground. The town, its springs discovered by goldminers in the 1850s, is positioned at the southern end of 40-mile long Harrison Lake, and in the early evening sunlight we walked along the sandy shoreline of an extremely pretty resort. A pity we couldn't spend more time here, but Vancouver Island was calling, and next morning we set off for the ferry terminal at Tsawwassen where Martin said his farewells, as he had to dash off to Seattle to make arrangements for the next tour, and we boarded the ferry.

Vancouver

The 2 hour crossing of a millpond-like Strait of Georgia brought us to land on Vancouver Island near Nanaimmo, from where we headed on to our night's stop at Englishman Falls Park, yet another wilderness campground, but near to some spectacular waterfalls within the woods. Our replacement wagonmaster, Sidney, joined us for the rest of the holiday and, after a quiet night, we were off early as we had to cross a mountain range to get to the Pacific side of the island.

At Coombs we toured the old country market, with goats grazing away on its grass-covered roof. At Cathedral Grove we wandered amongst giant 800 year-old Douglas Fir trees - up to 240 foot high - many now lying where they had fallen after the storms of 1997. At Port Alberni, renowned for its salmon fishing, we visited the quayside and dined in our 'van outside the souvenir shops which dotted the area. Then came the long trek on a narrow and very twisty road towards the Pacific Rim National Park, past the surf-swept sands of Long Beach, and into our eventual destination at Crystal Cove.

Two nights here gave us a last opportunity for sightseeing, this time a few miles along the road at Tofino. Some of our party were whale-watching there, so we hitched a lift with them into town, and visited the Eagle Aerie Gallery, where Roy Vickers displays his magical artwork, full of life and colour. We could not resist, and today 'The Two of Us' hangs on our wall as a reminder of our Canadian holiday. We watched sea-plane activity in the harbour, had a snack in a cyber-cafe, and missed the day's post before thumbing a lift back to camp... the bus timetable was somewhat optimistic.

That evening we wandered about the near-by beach as dusk fell, climbing the rocks to gaze out into the Pacific sunset before returning to our site, and our last evening's barbecue, capably hosted by Kenny and Sidney. A good note to finish on. Next morning it's up bright and early... it's around 140 miles back to the ferry terminal at Duke Point... and it's that dratted road again! We made it to Nanaimo for a refuel stop (the 'vans have to be returned as full as possible), then driving down to the ferry, which was not long in arriving. We were ready for this rest period, during which we said our farewells to those in our party who were driving the 28-footers; they had to be returned to Seattle in the USA. That left two motorhomes and our Wagonmaster Kenny to drive back to the Vancouver depot for our final handover, carried out efficiently and without incident... we had been fortunate in our journey of over 2600 kms not to have suffered any breakdown or accidental damage. From here, a minibus had been laid on to run us to the Abercorn Hotel in Richmond where we were to stay an additional three nights, taking the opportunity to look around Vancouver City before flying home.

Much has been written about Vancouver; how like a UK city it is... is that good?... and with a UK-type climate too! But it has to be seen to understand what a delightful place it really is, for tourists anyway. There is so much to see and do, and sensations to experience. One morning we caught a bus southwards to the Buddhist temple, an island of peace within a bustling environment. We asked for "transfer tickets", which allowed us not only to catch another bus within a designated period without further charge, but one which actuallly took us twice as far on the return, into Downtown itself.

Gas Town and Clock

Here we visited Gas Town, with its steam clock and wonderful shops, China Town, Canada Place from where cruise ships depart for Alaska, the Imax Theatre and Omnimax Theatres with their huge screens and breathtaking programmes, caught the skytrain to Science World - a hands-on heaven for kids which completely baffled us, and dined at a very pleasant Chinese restaurant overlooking the harbour, where ships and seaplanes buzzed busily about.

Science World

We also managed a trip on the free bus around Stanley Park, and later walked about the city centre, popping into shopping malls and big stores just to say we had been there. But there was still so much we were unable to see... the Harbour Centre Tower, Capilano Suspension Bridge, Grouse Mountain, the Botanical Gardens, Granville Island, ride on the ferry at False Creek... that we look forward to one day returning to Vancouver to pick up where where we left off; possibly another two weeks might just do it! But for this occasion, our thanks go to Escorted Motorhomes, who made the whole journey possible; it CAN be done without them, but for first-timers we would not hesitate to recommend them every time.

East German Tour
organised for SMOC by GB Privilege

12th June to 27th June 2005

Some rallies are good, some are great, and we thought that this trip in June to East Germany was one of the latter. Hosted by GB Privilege, who also provided the Tour Directors Ron and Sue Morgan, some 26 S.M.O.C. motorhomes set off by ferry from Dover to Calais on the first leg of the adventure. Most of us had not been to Germany before, and several were in fact first-time ralliers, and it was with some trepidation that we looked ahead to those days when getting some mileage under our wheels was the primary target. However, as the tour would really only begin once we had reached East Germany, initial long distances were a necessity, and the first night's stop-over at the Chateau du Grandspette some 30 miles South of Calais, allowed us to get to know one another - and our Tour Leaders also, at least a little.

Next day saw us heading for the motorway outside Dunkirk, and from there via Brussels to a very pleasant site by the Rhine at Remagen (remember the film?). We wandered down to see the remains of the bridge at that spot, now a very peaceful place with the sun highlighting the passage of several Rhine steamers. That evening we all congregated in the restaurant on site for our first included meal (viener schnitzel, what else?). We had got our longest journey (285 miles) out of the way, and it was a pity we couldn't stay on here longer, but East Germany was still calling, and the next day we were off again on the autobahns to a forest site south of Gotha on the A4. The access road is not likely to be forgotten, but once there we were staying two nights, and so able to gather ourselves together somewhat. After all, another 276 miles had been covered without mishap, and the oldest and slowest motorhome in the group (ours!) had kept up with the best.

The Bridge at Remagen

The weather was good, the roads in general OK, despite severe congestion around Cologne and several patches of major road construction. Ron had organised coffee and lunchtime breaks at some motorhome service stations for those who travelled with him in convoy (not all did all the time as 26 'vans makes a somewhat impressive-looking hazard for others) and after many miles of concentrated driving these were very welcome.

Our next site was a 3-night stopover at Camping Bad Sonneland, a little way outside Dresden. Although we were all crowded together under the trees it was a pleasant site, with a lake and a restaurant well patronised by several members of our party. Even better was the bus stop outside the site, and many of us took the opportunity to visit Dresden, with its centre full of old and beautiful buildings, yet still coming to terms with the ravages of Hitler's war. Like Coventry, it had been the target of sustained bombing, and one church had been restored but left undecorated as a memorial to those times.

A little up the road from the campsite was the small town of Moritzburg, with its very beautiful Castle, which some of us took the short bus ride there to visit. Built in the 16th century by the Duke of Saxony it stands in the middle of a lake and is joined to the mainland by its causeways.

Moritzburg Castle

Next day saw us visit the Meissen porelain factory, and then on to Colditz, a name which is still held in awe and another stark reminder of the tribulations of the last war. A guided tour showed us the conditions under which the prisoners-of-war lived, and glimpses into the many and various ways which they devised in their attempts to escape.

Back on the road again, and off to our next site, this time the Kladower Damm outside Berlin. From here we were given an all-day bus tour around some of the more famous spots such as the Olympic Stadium, built in 1936 and once the scene of Hitler's famous speeches and just remodelled for the World Cup next year (we got there first!), the Charlottenburg Schloss,

Unter den Linden, the Reichstag, the Brandenburg Gate, the remains of the Berlin Wall, and Checkpoint Charlie.

Olympic Stadium, Berlin

We were very impressed with the many open spaces in the city and with the new buildings, especially the Sony Centre, where we had another very enjoyable lunch. Over the next two days most of us were able to re-visit Berlin, some taking in a river cruise, and also to visit the adjacent city of Potsdam, all courtesy of an inclusive and very cheap ticket covering bus, ferry (across the Wannsee Lake), tram and train. Some even managed a lake cruise, or visited the Luftwaffe museum on the ex-airfield near to our site (and where one of our number had once been stationed in his time in the R.A.F.)

We were drawing near to the end of of a most enjoyable trip to Easr Germany, and the homeward journey lay towards the Hartz Mountains. Once more the autobahn came into use, until at Braunschweig those of us following our revered leader headed south towards Bad Harzburg. Here his navigator experienced some little difficulty, and we had a very pleasant - if unplanned - trip through the mountains before finally arriving at our destination from the other direction. Next day we had an included coach trip through the Hrtz Mountains, calling first at a cafe high above Goslar with superb views, and then for an included lunch at a restaurant in Torfhaus. Our journey back to site was delayed by an earlier accident, and during the wait our driver York entertained us with his Oh's and Ah's (arm movements included!).

Goslar Flea Market

Our final day we saw the first rain in the two weeks of our journey, but was not enough to put off a visit to the nearby fairy-like town of Goslar. Here were Gothic buildings, an impressive 'Rathaus' (town hall), a street market, a second-hand fair, a charity display by the local fire-fighters, and many ice-cream and cafe venues, as well as the usual tourist shops. That evening we gathered in the site's restaurant for our farewell meal, and with the (free) drinks flowing freely said our goodbyes. Next morning those motorhomes not staying on wandered off in dribs and drabs, some shooting off to the ferry with Ron and Sue, others taking the time and opportunity to move homeward by indirect routes. We had met many characters and made some new friends, who we look to see again at future rallies. It had, for us, been a great trip to an area of Europe which we probably would not have considered going to on our own. Although it had entailed a great deal of driving (on getting home by a reasonably short route we had done over 2200 miles in total), it had been great fun as well as very educational, and had certainly whetted our appetites for another visit to Germany.

Brian and Maureen Davies

A Visit To East Germany

June 2005

When offered the chance to join a motorcaravan group visiting East Germany, it was an opportunity too good to miss. The distances to be covered meant that, on our own, we would not have contemplated it. Although familiar with France and Spain, this area of Germany always seemed a step too far, but we are now very glad that we made the decision.

Although an escorted tour, the term was loosely applied, and the first couple of days was spent in pounding the motorways. We stopped at a site at Remagen (remember the film?) where the remains of the bridge are still to be seen on either side of the Rhine. Then on to a forest site at Gotha, and eventually - despite some horrendous traffic outside Cologne - to our very pleasant pre-booked site at Camping Bad Sonneland, outside Dresden. From here a bus ran into Dresden, where we spent a most interesting day.

It is rising once more from the ashes of its tremendous - and unnecessary - bombing by the R.A.F. on 13th February 1945. Much of the centre is being reconstructed in its original style, and sometimes it is hard to tell old from new. The cathedral, castle and the Zwinger Gardens are all worthy of a visit, and an outdoor lunch in the Altmarket was an experience. What *was* old (ancient?) was the Mercedes motorcaravan we came across, parked in a side street. Looked like a refugee from the Russian occupation!

In the other direction from the campsite was the small town of Moritzburg, with its very beautiful castle. Built in the 16th century by Duke Moritz of Saxony, and almost surrounded by water, it is home nowadays to international music festivals. We also visited - by coach - the Meissen porcelain factory, and then Colditz, a name still held in awe, which is more than can be said nowadays for the real thing.

Entrance to Colditz Castle

Its entrance glistened white in sunshine, and inside was considerable evidence of the castle's current conversion into pension-type accommodation. Still, a quick tour of the older parts showed us the conditions under which Second World

War P.O.W.s lived, and glimpses into the many and varied methods of escape they attempted.

Back on the road again our next site was at Kladower Damm outside Berlin. A pre-arranged all-day bus tour took us around some of the more famous spots. The Olympic Stadium, built for the 1936 Olympic Games, and subsequently the scene of Hitler's speeches, had just been remodelled for the World Cup this year.

Charlottenburg Schloss

Also visited was the Charlottenburg Schloss, the famous Unter den Linden, the Brandenburg Gate, the Reichstag, the remains of the Berlin Wall, and 'Checkpoint Charlie'. The many new buildings - including the new railway station under construction, and the Sony Centre - the abundant open spaces, and the river cruise, all impressed us greatly. Also from the site we were able to take the ferry across the Wansee Lake to Potsdam, where we took a tram trip around the city and visited the Sansoucci Palace and Orangerie, another Brandenburg Gate, and Brandenburger Street with its al fresco dineries (and out-of-this-world ice cream concoctions).

Outdoor dining in Potsdam

Our final pre-booked campsite was in the Hartz Mountains, at Bad Hartzburg, from where we took the bus into the fairy-like town of Goslar. Here were Gothic buildings, an impressive 'Rathaus' (Town Hall), a flea market and a charity display by the local fire-fighters, as well as the usual cafes and tourist shops. That evening at the farewell meal we said our goodbyes, and next day headed, quite slowly, for home. En route, we stayed at a campsite outside Hameln (Hamelin of Pied Piper fame) and that afternoon crossed the River Weser into the city. Outside the town hall a local group had put on a production of the Pied Piper that morning (which, sadly, we missed!). Much of the town centre is pedestrianised, and we found an outdoor seat at a cafe for our evening meal. A pleasant walk back to the site can include an interesting diversion onto the island in the river.

And so home... via Holland, Belgium, and a myriad motorways, to Calais. A recommended site is to the South at Guines. Get here early enough (we didn't) and you can use its swimming pool for free. Next morning we called at the Europa Centre and its supermarkets, to stock up... chiefly with wines of all kinds and prices. Then to the ferryport, and so home (more motorways, with far less provision for travellers than those on the Continent). Despite the many miles of driving (over 2200) we had really enjoyed the trip and seen many places which were only names before. Perhaps sometime we'll take our motorhome again that way, next time by ourselves. We've done it once, now for the T-Shirt!

Exploring the Massif Central

2005

We had crossed the English Channel on one of P & O's newest cruise ferries, the *Pride of Portsmouth*, and with a time of five hours thirty minutes we were soon approaching Le Havre in our Swift Kon-Tiki motorhome. We had been there before, when we had to cross the Tancarville Bridge but now the Pont du Normandie (toll 5 euros) was open, and we made our way across and south to the very pleasant site of La Route d'Or, across the river Loire and on the edge of La Fleche. In the evening the site laid on a visit from local dignitaries who, in the provided marquee, set before the campers assembled there the sights and delights of the area, including wine, cheese and nibbles.

After La Fleche we turned towards the Way of the Kings, alongside the Loire. Past Saumur, with its chateau brooding above the town, and the high cliffs riddled with caves, once used for bottling and storing wine. Then on past Chinon and on to the historic walled town of Richelieu, built by France's greatest cardinal to provide accommodation for his court. But we were aiming further and higher, for the Central Massif in the Auvergne. Creation of this area had commenced some 25 million years ago but many of the peaks are comparatively young, some dating from as recently as 7000 years ago. At last the region's mountains loomed ahead, and we could see our first target, Le Puy de Dome. If you have children with you do not miss Vulcania, which will give them a deeper insight into creation and working of volcanoes, for that is what the area is all about. An easy-to-find site is at the local sportsdrome in Orcines, the name derived from the Latin for bears.

One can usually drive to the top of Le Puy de Dome from the car-park, but not on weekends or holidays, so we let the Navette, or shuttle-bus, take the strain. We de-bussed by the cafe with its souvenir shop; the actual summit is topped by a television transmitting station, which can be seen from miles away. What cannot be so easily seen are the ruins of the Temple of Mercury, built by the Romans during their occupation, but only discovered in 1872. The view from up here is amazing; to the east we could see the city of Clermont-Ferrand, whilst south-west we gazed across the multitude of extinct volcanoes comprising the Chaine des Puys. That afternoon we opted to keep our feet on (relatively) level ground so made our way first to the village of Orcival. The Romanesque church of Notre Dame de Fer was once a shrine for escaped prisoners, its outside walls hung with manacles and leg-irons once in use on them. The near-by medieval village of the Grottes de Jonas is carved out of the softer volcanic rock known as tufa and during the 1-hour tour we clambered in and out of more than sixty rooms across four floors, joined by spiral staircases. Good stout shoes are required for this sort of exercise.

Next day we took the road on to St. Flour, finding a site just as we entered the town. Be careful here, Les Orgues is poorly signed, and one has to wait outside the entrance until the gardienne can raise the height barrier. Once in, however, the pitches are large and well-spaced, the facilities good and the view excellent. We were near enough to the Upper town to be able to leave one's vehicle and walk in, so next morning we spent an interesting hour walking cobbled medieval streets, sampling Auvergne delicacies and avoiding the lure of souvenirs and beautiful clothes. Our way out of town lay downhill, passing on the right the strange rock-face of organ-pipes known as orgues. One can make for the A75 motorway, but we preferred to use the D909 which takes one to the spectacular view of the Viaduc-du-Garabit. This carries the railway across a series of u-bends on the roadway as it climbs out of the valley. Turning left just before these we began our trek across an area better known in July 1944 for its serious resistance activity and the heavy retribution taken on the Maquis. The D589 ploughs steadily east through the Margeride mountains, where at frequent intervals - especially around Clavieres - can be seen the many roadside crosses and inscriptions to the dead fighters. If one wishes, divert along the forest road towards Mont-Mouchet, and view the local and national memorials set up to honour them.

At Sauques we pulled into the parking lot of the local sports arena for our lunch, stopping next to a huge wooden carved stature of a St. James pilgrim pointing back along the way to Compostela in north-west Spain. Here too was the first petrol station since St. Flour, so we thankfully topped up and went on towards our eventual goal, Le Puy-en-Velay, capital of this very volcanic region and home of the famous Puy lentils. The municipal campsite lies on the northern edge of the medieval city, and almost at the foot of one of its striking volcanic plugs pointing heavenwards. Its 85 metres are surmounted by the 14th century church of St. Michel d'Aiguille. Do not neglect to climb its 300 steps to see the amazing frescoes recently discovered, and to take in the view across the city. Nearby too is the Corneille Rock, crowned by a huge bronze statute of Our Lady, cast in 1860 from guns captured at Sebastopol. We were within walking distance of the ancient city centre, and visited the cathedral, climbing the narrow cobbled street to its magnificent medieval frontage. All along the street can be seen producers and sellers of the lace for which the city is renowned. Inside the church it was very noisy and we saw a number of pilgrims who were obviously receiving blessings and making final preparation for their long trek to Santiago de Compostela. Some were dressed poorly, sporting the shell, emblem of the pilgrims, and clutching their staff, eyes firmly on the journey ahead.

The gorges of the river Tarn lie not too far away to the south-west, so it was down the N88 towards Mende, diverting at Langogne to visit the Barrage de Naussac, both a reservoir and a haven for water-sports enthusiasts. A little further on we became aware of silhouettes of people standing by the roadside, a novel and thought-provoking way of drawing attention to road casualties in the area. After Balsieges we took the direct route south across the bleak and barren Causse de Sauveterre, but with a beauty of its own. Eventually we turned sharply downhill and were amazed to see, hundreds of feet almost vertically below us, the small but very busy medieval settlement of St.Enimie. The descent is not for the faint of heart, nor is it recommended to try out of the siesta period; the steep and narrow twisting road would make the passing of two large vehicles very hazardous, as only a small stone wall separated us from a nasty drop. At the bottom we headed first for the car park but, being siesta time still, it was full of vehicles, many with canoe racks fixed behind them. The Tarn here is noted for its water activities, canoeing being right at the top, so we moved downriver a bit and parked up to watch the canoeists as they paddled past, aiming no doubt for one of the many campsites alongside the river catering for them.

Church of Saint Michael d'Aiguilhe, Le Puy

Chateau de Val & Vedettes

Boardwalk in Puy de Sancy

Entrayques

Main Street, le Bourboule

Saint Enemie

The drive down the D907 through the gorge is an exercise of concentration in order that the driver might safely appreciate its impressive grandeur. At the same time one must avoid collision with other vehicles on the narrower stretches, and in places a swerve towards the river bank may be necessary in order to pass safely beneath overhanging rock. There are also occasional tunnels where being able to see around corners would be very advantageous. In the end, of course, we journeyed successfully and arrived late afternoon for our overnight stop at "Les Cerisiers e Pailhas", a well-set out campsite a little before Aguessac, on the river bank - and in the middle of a cherry orchard. We were welcomed by the owners with a cooling drink before signing in and setting 'Connie' down for the night; ten euros and well worth it! The well-provisioned camp shop also sold ice cream, post cards and...cherries. Chips and pies were also available.....must have known the English were in the area. Bathers and sunbathers were still down by the river, making the most of the warm evening sunshine.

We had reached our furthest point south and now we were, gradually, heading home, but there was much yet to do and to see. After Espalion the road runs through the Gorges du Lot to Entraygues, but the scenery did not match up to that of the Tarn so we continued northwest to Aurillac. We had read of a campsite some ten miles west of the city at Lacapelle - Viescamp, and next to a lake. It was very hot, and the water beckoned so we gave it a try. The lake had, unfortunately, once been a gravel quarry and the ground, both in and out of the water, was hard and gritty, so we returned to site and made use of its very attractive swimming pool. Next morning it was back to Aurillac and on to Mauriac and Bort-les- Orques (the organ pipes again!). Here we found the municipal site ,with ample space and a gardian who not only made us very welcome but, before retiring for the night, wished us all a pleasant stay in the area and safe onward journey on his public address system - in good English. Next morning we visited the Barrage de Orgues, a huge concrete wall belonging to the EDF, who produce electricity here; above the dam is a large artificial lake, the result of flooding these reaches of the Dordogne. The 15th century fairy-tale castle of Chateau de Val, once on a rocky crag high above the valley, now stands romantically on a small island, reached by a causeway. An outside stone staircase leads to the main door and a worthwhile visit to the furnished rooms and a permanent exhibition of contemporary art. From the exterior parapet walk one has a splendid panoramic view over the lake. An hour-long cruise on a vedette (pleasure-boat) took us to almost the lake's northern point. Unfortunately the only on-board commentary is in French, so we must have missed quite a bit as the guide never stops talking! However, a leaflet in English (available if you ask) tries hard.

Our site for the next couple of days was Le Poutie at la Bourboule, some twenty miles further on where - it being the eve of Bastille Day - we opted for a two-night stay. This pleasant three-star campsite is inexpensive, has a swimming pool, and pitches separated into small groups. La Bourboule is a 19th century spa town straddling the infant Dordogne, and people - especially children - with allergies and respiratory complaints come from all over for the cure. It was a beautiful day, so we made the half-hour walk into the town. People were everywhere enjoying themselves. The two main streets are parallel and either side of the river, so there is a feeling of space, with the mountains providing a dramatic backdrop. Enthralled and well-behaved children were seated in front of a stage, being played to by jugglers and entertainers. We walked out to the Parc de Fenestre on the edge of the town, with its lake, miniature railway, extremely large enclosed playground catering for all ages of children, and a cable car to lift the visitor to the Plateau de Charlannes. All around were people, many of them children and teenagers, enjoying themselves in the sunshine, with no dropped litter or unseemly behaviour in evidence. One could not help but compare -unfavourably - our own towns and amenities.

The highest peak in the Auvergnes is le Puy de Sancy but first we dropped in at le Mont Dore, another of the many spa towns of the area. The more impressive buildings to the north of the town seemed chiefly devoted to "Les Thermes". As everywhere, shops closed at 12 noon, but we noticed bread (the long type) being purchased from a vending machine. Then up the D983 into the Cirque de Sancy, and after lunch booked ourselves into the "telepherique", which takes one only part way to the summit; one has to negotiate a boardwalk and climb over 720 steep wooden steps to reach it. From here (at 6,130 feet) we had stupendous views back over the town, and south to Lac Pavin, a flooded volcanic crater. Back at the cable-car station it was coffee and crepes to warm us up before descending past impressive rocky crags and outcrops to 'Connie', and on to the campsite at Les Bombes. There was adequate space here, so it was strange to see a long line of motorhomes, mainly French, camped down the lane outside the site. Apparently this is an accepted practice, and a water, disposal and electric point (a "borne" - usually operated by a token) was available for their use just outside the main gate..

We were now on our final lap home, but wanted to visit the cities of Bourges and Vendome, so we took the D982 from Ussel and, by-passing Aubusson , made for Montlucon.. If you don't know the location of the municipal site in Bourges - don't bother to ask. No-one else seems to either, and local by-laws apparently prohibit the use of signs to get you there. And it wasn't shown on *our* map of the city. However, the site is worth the effort and although at 15 euros (incl. electricity) was the most expensive of all we had come across, had good facilities and was within easy walking distance of the medieval centre. That evening we walked up past fountains dancing in the dusk to the floodlit gothic cathedral of St. Etienne, famous for its five doorways.

.

From Bourges, both Tours and Orleans are within striking distance but we preferred to make for Vendome, a town - and site - to which we had been many years before. However, this did not stop us missing our way as we approached the city on the D957. Taking - by mistake - a steep and narrow descent we suddenly found ourselves in the town's market place, and only a quick guess correctly took us out and along past the church to the gates of Camping des Grandes Pres. The 5-acre campfield is dotted with trees for shade, and lies alongside the river Loir. That evening we saw a long table laid under an awning, with many people eating there, and only later found out that this was a dining occasion open to all, on payment of a modest fee. We'll remember that next time! We also discovered that entry to the adjacent swimming pool, with its sun terraces and cafe, was free to campers on production of a pass, which we promptly obtained and made good use of the following morning.

This really was the final lap, and we headed north to Chartres, and on past Dreux and Evreux to Rouen. The route here lies along Boulevade le Havre. but road signage is pathetic, and careful map-reading is the order, else one can drift unaware onto the motorway. The D982 alongside the Seine is a pleasant and quiet route towards the port, and soon after passing under the Pont de Tancarville we finished the journey in style on the A131. Next morning was an early start and by 8.30 am we had boarded P & O's *Pride of Le Havre* and was heading out of the harbour. The end of another not-to-be-forgotten visit to France, as had been all our others. What a land of memories France is for us. Next year....who knows?

To Florence and Pisa in a Nexxo

2008

Purchased from new in May of last year, it drove like a dream and coped well with the Italian mountains and the autoroutes alike. The price of diesel abroad was somewhat less than here in the U.K., and unmanned fuel pumps were available and no problem to use with a credit card. Going south we had a deadline to meet so used the peages quite a bit to save time. In Italy we had planned NOT to use them but travelling through the small coastal towns was fraught with a great many hazards, and going into large cities was not an option, so again the autostrada came to our rescue more than once, albeit at a cost. The motorways all correctly charged us for Class 2, and in over three and half thousand miles I saw only one speed camera (there may have been others but we tried not to look too hard). Our only known transgression was in a tunnel (there were so many of them) on the autostrada above Genoa, where we were soundly berated by an Italian work truck - I had neglected to turn the headlights back on, an offence the police hadn't been there to spot. And, oh yes, if you are on the A4 autostrada towards Turin, and wish to continue westwards, do NOT take the signed route to the city and head for Collegno instead. This will take you around Turin towards France or Switzerland via the A32. WE ended up well and truly lost in the city, found ourselves in the market area with its tramlines and narrow streets, and only extricated ourselves when we spotted a sign to the Susa gateway, otherwise we might still be there! The city centre is restricted access, so another transgression we were fortunate to get away with.

Before setting off I had invested in the ACIS handbook of campsites. Travelling largely in the off-season we took advantage of the discounts (10,12 or 14 euros a night) which the book offered us at selected sites. These varied between small family-owned ones to larger ones with full entertainment facilities, but all were well run and most welcoming. We saved over 100 euros by using these during our five weeks abroad. One French site also appears in the Castels Guide and, as it happened, we arrived on the day France was playing Holland in the European Cup. There were many Dutch campers on site so the owner (French) pleased us all by putting on a dinner so that we could all watch the game in the chateau on her large-sized TV screen. The dinner was good and the result (to us) was immaterial. Be warned however....if you turn up at one of the larger campsites between one and three o'clock you may well have to wait outside until they re-open, although walking around to choose your pitch in advance may be permitted. Much of such sites are devoted to permanent enclaves, with caravan, wooden shed, gazebo and awning all playing their part in making up the Italian holiday home. During the evening walkabout we could see large family groups enjoying their meals, with the ubiquitous televisions blaring in the background. The standard of hygiene at these campsites was high and we were fascinated by the Italian practice of returning from their shower dressed in all-enveloping terry-towelling, and hooded like monks. At many sites in Italy too it is mandatory for all swimmers (including children) to wear a bathing cap which, if you do not bring your own, can be purchased on-site for a couple of euros. Nearly all sites boasted one or more pools, and we made good use of them. Camping Michaelangelo, above Florence, and our most expensive site at 34 euros a night, was with no pool an exception, and we found it hard to remain cool in 40 degrees whilst waiting for evening, when we took the bus from outside the site gate for a late foray into the city.

A further word of caution. We had arrived in Pisa around midday and decided to park at a convenient supermarket on the edge of the city. There were a number of cars there, plus three other motorhomes. I had forgotten that some supermarkets close for up to three hours at lunchtime, and on our return from a walk into Pisa found that most of the cars, and two of the motorhomes, had by now departed. This relative desertion had been taken advantage of by two young men who, despite our vehicle alarm loudly sounding, had forced their way into our 'van, regrettably destroying all three locks in the process, and were busy investigating and about to remove any valuables they might come across. Stupidly, I had left our U.K. money, spare euros and passports in a wallet under a seat and which they had found but not yet opened. Our trying to apprehend the man at the rear window gave the other time to step out of the main door and they both hurried away faster than we could move. On a quick inspection of the chaos left as they sorted through our belongings showed that we had returned just in time, and nothing had in fact been stolen. I returned to the city centre to report the break-in to the police but, being lunchtime, none were available. Even when I stopped a cruising carabinieri they were not interested....no injury plus no theft equalled, to them, no crime. C'est la vie, or whatever the Italian equivalent is. I promptly learned my lesson and put ALL valuables into the onboard safe, thanking the gods for our deliverance. Fortunately, all three locks still worked from the inside, but it did mean that when leaving the 'van one door had to remain unlocked for our re-entry.

On our return journey through France we took the opportunity to call on friends in the Ardeche area and spent four days on the municipal site at La Valette, near to St. Ambroix. This site would benefit from a general tidy-up but is otherwise well-equipped with a large pool and restaurant and is handily placed for the supermarket and railway station in nearby Bessages. From here we look the train to Ales. a pleasant town on the

Gardon river, and which boasts a semi-derilict Vauban fortress. We lunched at a pavement cafe, and then called at the local Orange/France telecom shop in the town as our 'phone credit was running low. We had hoped to top it up but discovered that this cannot be done abroad. The shop was similarly unenlightened until they tried it. Then "sorry, but's an English 'phone". I had already told them that, but they still had tried to load it with 20 euros. Their suggestion was to buy a French SIM card (at 28 euros) then load THAT with credit, but that would only last a month, when any unused credit would be wiped.

Of the 31 European sites used, we would heartily commend half a dozen as value-for-money in terms of prices charged, welcomes and facilities. In France, C des Princes d'Orange at Orpierre (a mediaeval village near to Serres) was worth the 6km diversion. Domaine de Labellier at St. Victor de Malcap near to St.Ambroix is large and well-equipped, with all pitches under trees. In Italy, River Camping at Amelgia near to La Spezia, Camping Europa at Torre de Lago Puccini near Viareggio, Il Serjente near the Passo della Futa on the SR65, and La Tranquilla above Baveno on Lake Maggiore (try the boat on the lake if you can find time - it offers unlimited travel and landings for a day trip). There were of course other good sites, but they either didn't offer the discount at all or we were into High Season (July). At a couple of sites in France we *were* able to negotiate a lower price, but this practice is rare. However, the site at Lake Garda (C. Serenella) is on the lakeside, and those at Frejus (Pont d'Argens) and Sottomarina (Miramare) on the Adriatic are right next to the sea, so there were compensations.

Florence

Fountain at Ales

On Lake Magiore

Pisa's leaning tower

And finally....when planning, or making, your trip abroad be sure you have a good and up-to-date campsite guide. Mine for Northern France was dated 1994 and while most campsites (especially municipal ones) tend to go on and on, the Municipal at Bethune didn't. Although well-signposted, we discovered that it had been closed down quite a while previously, with the entry blocked off by boulders. Someone please tell the Maire, preferably in French, to remove its signs. And at Aire-sur-la-Lys the site seems to have disappeared altogether. We eventually ended up at the Chateau du Gandspette (good but expensive at 27 euros) in the village of Eperleques. Still, it did enable us to visit the remains of the nearby German "blockhaus" from where 'flying bombs' - V1's - and rockets - V2's - were intended to be launched at England. Another day, and we could have visited a similarly impressive war museum at near-by La Coupole, outside St. Omer.

The trip, apart from our stays with friends in the south of France, consisted mainly of travelling, so we gave both ends of the vehicle a good use. The cab end performed very well and, apart from difficulty in reading the digital screen on the move, was a joy to drive after our manual 18-year-old Kontiki. Although fitted with cruise control, opportunities to make use of it were limited, due chiefly to the number of heavy lorries on the autostradas. The living quarters are quite adequate for two, although we at times missed the freedom our old Kontiki had given us to move around. Still, the absence of a long settee did mean I had to be tidier than before, no more dropping clothes and magazines/books where I sat. The larger and more easier-operated 'fridge was much appreciated, as was the built-in bed...no more shuffling of seats and cushions about. We are now looking forward to camping in our Nexxxo in this country although, with diesel in both France and Spain quite a bit cheaper, we may all be spending our motoring holidays on the continent. And that would hit hard our own economy.

A Yorkshire Odyssey

2009

Taking advantage of the fine weather following this year's Wimbledon, little time was lost in getting our Burstner Nexxo motorhome ready for its second big run-out this year….we had already taken a three-week jaunt to Normandy and Brittany in March, during the last spell of fine weather. Having business to attend to in Peterborough, our first night was spent at the Caravan Club's well-equipped Ferry Meadows site. This suited us as we were en route anyway to the North of England showground at Pickering via Kirmington, where Timberland were to replace a wardrobe door damaged during fitting-out, before crossing the Humber bridge. Then we were really on holiday, and spent our first night at Inholmes Lodge, a Caravan Club CL at Beeford. The next few days saw us wandering, literally, around North Yorkshire, on a somewhat unplanned route. We tried, unsuccessfully, to find the castle at Skipsea, so pressed on to Bridlington, where we encountered our first parking problem. The car park at the south end of the town is adjacent to the cliffs, and indeed uses a stretch of the land there, but the entrance had the ubiquitous height barrier and, for a moment, we were stumped. Adjacent however is the car park reserved for boat-owners and, taking pity on us perhaps, we were allowed to park there for a couple of quid. This gave us ample time to take the road train into the town, and to wander, as you do, before walking back to the 'van. What the thinking is behind the council's decision is to me a mystery….do they not want motorhomes visiting their town? In the end we headed off to Flamborough Head, before making our way to the Caravan Club's limited facility site at Rosedale, a very lovely setting even if the road to it out of Pickering was somewhat of an adventure.

Golden Square Campsite, nr Helmsley

Next day was show day, where we tried hard not to spend anything…and managed it too. The last time we went to a show of that kind we bought a new motorhome, so we were rather circumspect this time, and anyway the weather didn't help greatly. We got a place for the night at Golden Square campsite (great for families) outside Helmsley, and next morning visited Helmsley Castle, which had been partially destroyed during the Civil War. One owner since that time was a London banker, Sir Charles Duncombe, who built the adjacent Duncombe House. Following the then fashion he wanted a picturesque ruin on his property to impress friends, and so the castle was never restored. Next to Rievaulx Abbey a short ride away, the first Cistercian Abbey in Northern England. After its dissolution under Henry 8th it fell into the hands of the Earl of Rutland, who promptly began the destruction of the buildings. Adjacent to its substantial remains is a shop and café, where we took the opportunity to lunch before setting off across the Hambleton Hills towards Osmotherly. This is not a trip for the fainthearted and, if I had known what it entailed, would not have attempted it. Still, due to an absence of head-on traffic for most of the way we managed it safely….this time…and were able to set down for the night at the Cote Ghyll campsite just out of the village.

Helmsley Castle

We generally use the Phillips Navigator roadmap to plan our route (or to see where we have got to…no SatNav, see!,… and a campsite site shown within the boundaries of Middlesbrough seemed to offer us a chance to visit that town for the first time. If you are tempted to do the same…don't bother. Although there are adequate signs to the site, it is just a piece of cindered land on the edge of an open space….no facilities, no security, and with the noise and worry of a skateboard park next to it. Apparently there used to be a warden living in the adjacent bungalow, but he/she is long gone. Why the site is shown on the map, and campers are still directed to it by signage, is yet another imponderable. So off to Whitby and the abbey there, founded in 657 by St. Hilda, a Saxon princess, and destroyed in 1538 by Henry 8th during the Dissolution of the Monasteries. Leaving the area we drove south past Scarborough, and did try for a site en route, but were told that bookings were only being taken for two-nighters as it was now peak season. We didn't take up their offer...their loss.... and spent the night at Lebberston Touring Park, with the nearby village pub giving us a change from self-catering.

The beach at Filey

With the weather still holding fair we headed again for the seaside, this time Filey, with its wide expanse of sands and the donkeys. Here the council provides very adequate parking at the far end of town, and it is a pleasant walk past the boating lake and through the gardens along the cliff-edge into town. On the way back we popped into the cliffside café for sustenance, before pressing on and down the notorious Sutton Bank...note, no caravans allowed here...and we saw why. Thirsk was market day, so that was that (no parking anywhere), and we ended up for the evening at the Riverside Meadows site outside Ripon. It is one of the "Flowers of May" group but, despite its size and a large entertainment centre with bar, seemed unable to provide meals…a pity that. It is also, in comparison, a most expensive site for us tourers, though no doubt families there for a week or more do get value from it.

Fountains Abbey

We passed through Ripon next morning, thinking we would return if there was time. In the event there wasn't, as we were now headed for Fountains Abbey. This proved a full day out, and included the tour around Studley Royal Water Garden, rightly a World Heritage site. Although in the care of the National Trust, and so free to members, it is also free to members of English Heritage, a point well worth noting. The initial minibus ride only took us to St. Margaret's Church, and was followed by a two-hour "stroll" through the gardens and on along the riverside back to the Abbey, very pleasant on a fine day. We were lucky to be at the Surprise View (the only cover on the way) when the heavens opened, but the sun soon came out again and we left with the feeling of a day well spent. So off to our overnight stop, this time at Woodhouse Farm, again well peopled with families. Not knowing where we would have reached any evening we had not booked any site other than Rosedale, and at times it took three or four calls before we found a suitable site at a reasonable (or not) rate. Still, it all adds to the fun and mystery of the holiday.

Brimham Rocks

When our children were still at junior school we had taken them to Brimham Rocks in Nidderdale, so we were keen to revisit the site and revive old memories. Apart from car parking (the only charge) now being provided by the National Trust, and a surfeit of greenery which at times blocked off the views, we were pleasantly surprised. True, I couldn't now scramble about on the rocks as I used to, but at least this gave me more time to appreciate the strange and fantastic shapes the rocks had assumed over time. Then on to Pateley Bridge, that rather quaint but attractive hillside town on the way to Grassington, before stopping the night at Wharfedale, the Caravan Club site at Long Ashes.

Gordale Scar Falls

Leaving the site next morning we turned off the B6265 at Cracoe, and followed the long and winding (and narrow) road, vicious stone walls on every side, through Airton to Kirkby Malham. Do NOT think of taking a caravan along this road….passing places are few and short. We had hoped to visit Malham itself, but after the Visitor Centre turned off first to visit Gordale Scar along another hair-raising road. Fortunately the tractors were still in the fields, and we reached the campsite without mishap. This is a relatively basic site, without electricity, but having toilet and washing facilities, though regrettably not in sufficient quantity to satisfy the very considerable number of campers who were there that day. There is no hardstanding, and the grassy surface was in places quite squishy. Still, it was perfect weather, blue sky and no clouds, so after setting up we walked the short distance along the path into the Scar itself. Walkers were scrambling up and down the waterfall rocks, whilst real climbers were using rope, piton and karabiner in their not very serious efforts to climb the adjacent near-vertical rock faces. After lunch we set off along the hill path towards Malham, but it was getting so hot that we gave up and returned to camp, consoling ourselves after dinner with a final walk into the Scar, and watching the sheep in the fields about settling down for the night.

Entrance to Gordale Scar

Next morning dawned with the eight-o'clock patter of raindrops on the camper roof. Remembering the state of the ground about, and the site owner's comment about pulling us off by tractor if need be, I lost no time in persuading our motorhome to navigate the short stretch of squishy ground and reach the pathway. Never have I seen so perfect an evening deteriorate into so foul a morning, and we were soon off the site and breakfasting by the side of the road. The rain grew in intensity, and we left the area wondering just how many motorhomes would require the tractor services on offer. Aiming for Clitheroe we stopped to view Sawley Abbey, but it was still raining so viewing was done from the comfort of the camper. The forecast promised no respite from rain and cloud so, feeling we had used up our luck as far as the weather gods were concerned, we headed homeward. And we were right; to date there has been little overall improvement in the weather. Where, oh where, are the promised "barbecue days" of this year's summer? Where indeed? And to think we had stayed in the UK this year instead of swanning off to sunny continental campsites. So, next year……

Whitby from the Abbey

A Quick Look at Lancaster

2013

Travelling north up the M6 motorway, away from the industrial conurbation of Manchester towards the idyllic peace of the English Lake District, one can break one's journey at junction 34 and drive westwards into the county town of Lancaster. From here one has easy access to Morecambe, Carnforth and Heysham, with Morecambe Bay to the west and the Forest of Bowland lying to the east. Lancaster itself is situated on a hill overlooking the original settlement, with the river Lune…from where the town derives its name…flowing south-west towards the sea.

Lancaster Castle

Lancaster Castle itself dates from Roman times, and boasts a dark and turbulent history. Initially its purpose was to face down the marauding tribes of Picts and Scots; since those days its history has encompassed scenes of religious persecution and the incarceration and punishment of countless criminals found guilty of such crimes as murder, theft, witchcraft and even membership of a Trades Union. Public hangings on the moors overlooking the town were rife, and some 200 individuals were dispatched here before these hangings were relocated to the castle itself. Nowadays the town is part of the Duchy of Lancaster, but prior to 1265 the castle was in the hands of Simon de Montfort, Earl of Leicester. However, in that year King Henry 3rd gave the settlement to his son Edmund, and in 1351, on Edmund's death, it passed to Edmund's grandson Henry Grosmont and became a County Palatine, so giving Henry, now a Duke), powers that would normally be in the hands of the king alone.

Brian and Maureen outside the castle

Henry died in 1362 without a male heir, so the title and inheritance passed to his daughter Blanche, to form part of her dowry in her marriage to one of Edward 3rd's sons, John of Gaunt. One result from all this is that our Queen Elizabeth has, like all our monarchs, title to the Duke of Lancaster

In the 18th century the dominant trades included cotton, tea, wood (notably mahogany) and spices from the Orient, and even slaves, enabled by the many merchants who saw that great profit was to be made in shipping. Large houses were constructed in Lancaster as homes for these merchants, whilst those who could not afford such luxury nevertheless housed themselves in smaller but no less comfortable settlements and villages outside the town. One such place, now but a speck on the map, was Sunderland (no, not that one), its name giving clue as to a broken (sundered) and separated place. But back then Sunderland Point, at the very mouth of the river Lune, was in a favoured position; from there merchants could await their "ship coming in" and so be amongst the first to reap their profits in Lancaster as their cargoes were unloaded. Indeed, it is claimed that the first cargo of cotton to enter Britain was landed here. Early on the harbour was designated as an 'outport' for Lancaster and a substantial pier and wharves were constructed by Robert Lawson, a wealthy and philanthropic Quaker. However, in 1728 Lawson went bankrupt, commencing the steady decline of the area and the inevitable growth of Glasson Docks on the opposite bank of the river.

Glasson Dock

Today, all that remains is a collection of mainly old houses, many converted from the original warehouses and businesses which once lined the frontage. And at the end of the village roadway can be found "Sambo's Grave", the resting place of a young black slave brought to England by a wealthy trader but then abandoned here as his master continued his travels, When Sambo died the villagers decided to bury him in an unconsecrated grave at its furthest point. So passed Sambo, and the glory which here once held an important place in the trading history of our nation.

The Ashton Memorial, Lancaster

Mediterranean Cruising

2013

We all know what cruises entail! Opulence, on-board swimming pools, sunbeds by the hundred, overeating and drinking (24 hours a day), and of course luxury cabins. Then there's all-day entertainment, fantastic evening shows in the ship's theatre, gaming machines, arts and craft demonstrations, competitions…the list is endless. So, let's get on with the actual journey, shall we?

We had decided some months before the actual day that it required something different, something more special, in the way of a celebration of my 80th birthday. After all, one never knows when the next one will come along! So we researched the field and decided that a nice leisurely cruise would suit the occasion admirably, and found one which would cover the actual day in question.

A newspaper ad. for Cruise Club showed that the 'Celebrity Eclipse' would be sailing from Southampton for the western Mediterranean. It would be the largest ship we had ever been on, with 2850 passengers and around 1500 crew….about one for every two passengers. We had our own stateroom attendant, who cleaned, tidied and provided as necessary. Our luggage magically appeared there, so no lugging of it.

The Celebrity Eclipse

It took two days of leisurely cruising –even through the Bay of Biscay – to reach our first port of call, Malaga. Here the sun shone warmly, and we were able to go ashore and visit one of Spain's premier cities. Being very familiar with it, we took our own time to enjoy a walkabout and tapas, and a visit to the cathedral before rejoining the ship some hours later.

Dining out in Malaga

The overnight trip took us to Villefranche, the port for Nice. It is not a deepwater harbour so we had to be landed by tender. We had opted for a coach trip here, which took us first to Nice itself (where we came across ex-President Sarcozy dining out), then on to Eze (nice and easy, we said!). At Eze we climbed up to the old town and the castle by way of narrow streets, before the return journey to the waiting boats., and on that evening to Italy.

The Colosseum, Rome

Next morning we had an opportunity to go by coach to Rome. On arrival in a huge underground coach park we joined 'millions' of others in St. Peter's Square in front of the Vatican. It proved impossible to get near without hours of waiting, so we contented ourselves with photos of the Vatican and the Sistine chapel. We then rejoined the coach for a very interesting tour around the tourist spots of the city…..the Colosseum, the Forum, the Palazzo Venezia (once Mussolini's H.Q.), Castel St. Angelo (variously a fortress, prison and palace), the Spanish Steps and many others.

When in Rome, the sun had shone all day, but next day dawned wet and windy as we approached Livorno, the port for Pisa and Florence. We had previously visited these places and had not booked for the trip to either city, retaining the option to visit the port area instead. However, in the event the weather kept us on board. This was the day that the big cycle race was taking place in Florence, and the rain simply poured down, so much so that the race was almost abandoned (and the British cyclists pulled out anyway). We were glad to have stayed put that day.

The pool area aboard the ship

Next morning saw us passing the Lantern at the edge of the port before anchoring at Genoa, the birthplace of Columbus. The city is on the doorstep so we were able to walk into it, passing the many market stalls lining the quayside. The city centre is compact and we easily found the Cathedral St. Lorenzo with its black-and white marble façade. Inside is a small chapel housing the bones of John the Baptist. We found Genoa to be a very pleasant city for a tourist to visit.

In Genoa harbour

Then followed a day at sea, before we saw on the horizon the towering outcrop of the British colony of Gibraltar. We thought we would do the "tourist" thing, so took a taxi from the harbour to the Rock.

At the top of Gibraltar

We stopped off at St. Michael's Cave, limestone caverns at 900 feet above sea level. Then on to the Ape's Den, where the 'monkeys' posed for photographs and begged for food, before calling in at the Siege Tunnels. These were blasted out of the rock during the siege of 1779-83, and are a tribute to the defenders who constructed and manned them all those years ago. Our taxi dropped us back at the beginning of the main shopping street, and we wandered slowly down past the Governor's residence, sadly boarded up for renovation at the time of our visit. After a street-side coffee we took advantage of a 'Hole-in-the-Wall' to get some U.K. cash. It was only later we realised it has issued us with Gibraltar notes, not viable in the U.K., so we called in at M & S to do a bit of shopping and to change those notes back into ones we could spend once back home.

Shopping in Gibraltar

Back at the dockside we enjoyed a cold towel and a fizzy drink before boarding the ship for our next – and last-stop, Lisbon. A city which we had never visited. The approach is by way of the river Tagus, narrow at first then opening out into a huge lagoon. Processing upriver we passed the 5-storey Belem

Tower, built in the early 1500's to deter pirates, but later serving as a prison. Then to the 25th April Bridge, the world's 3rd longest suspension bridge, and under which we had just a metre to spare, before docking at Tobacco Quay.

Celebrity Eclipse in harbour at Lisbon

After waiting some twenty minutes for a tour bus, on arrival it was full, so we cut our losses and walked into and up to the Old City. Here the streets are cobbled, and walking is hard on the feet. Fortunately we discovered a lift which took us much of the way towards the Castle of St. George, and to a café selling coffee (or chocolate) and pasteis de nata, an egg-based Portugese delicacy. Tourists are also carried about by small trolleybuses of various hues and ages, which rattle around on the narrow, steep and twisty cobbled streets, lending an air of old-world charm to the ancient city. From a viewpoint on the city's southern edge we were able to overlook the river and appreciate both the height we were at and the size of our ship anchored below, truly amazing. On the way back to the ship we came across a shop selling…port, of course.

Evening entertainment on board the Celebrity Eclipse

That night, our last on board, was nostalgic. As always, the evening show was great, leaving us with memories of a truly fantastic fortnight on the high seas. This had been our first major cruise, and tomorrow morning we would be docking at Southampton, saying our farewells and heading home. Next year....who knows?

Maureen's Cruise Diary

21st September - 6th October 2013

Mediterranean Cruise on Celebrity Eclipse

Saturday 21st September

We left Knighton at 10:15am after putting diesel in the car at Harry Tuffins.

We stopped for coffee at the Three Shires Garden Centre, Newent. It was a pleasant journey avoiding motorways - Gloucester, Cirencester, Romney to Southampton. It took us some time to find the Travel Lodge then we checked in and bought a £3 car parking for 24 hours. We took our luggage up to our room, 503.

On the journey we stopped in a lay-by to eat our picnic.

At 5:30pm we drove to The Balmoral, a Beefeater restaurant on Romney Road. Brian's meal was free with a birthday voucher. We shared a dessert - chocolate profiteroles with cream. We chose a different way back to the hotel, where we watched Casualty.

It took me about 2 hours to go to sleep, even though the bed was very comfortable - busy road. Awakened at 3:30am by noisy people in the street.

First look at the Celebrity Eclipse

View inside the cruise ship

Sunday 22nd September

Cruise Start

Ate our boxed breakfast in our room - I was not very impressed.

Arrived at Dock Gate 10 at approximately 10:30, Dock Gate 8 unavailable because of the Boat Show. Arrived on board 11:30 and greeted with a glass of champagne. up to deck 14 for buffet lunch in Oceanview Restaurant.

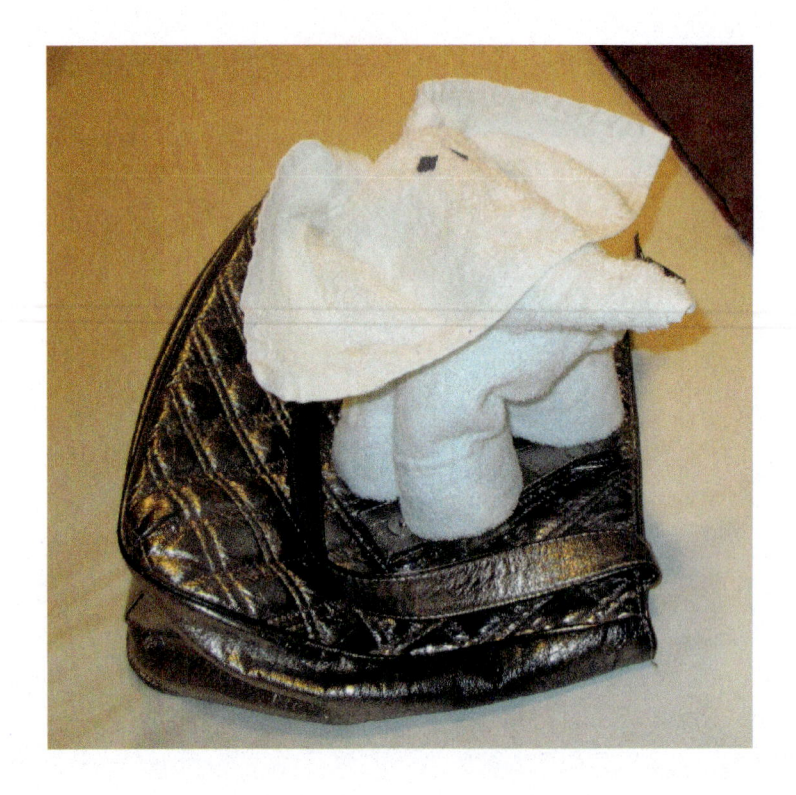

Elephant arrangement to the flannel and towel

1:30pm to our inside stateroom. But as our luggage wouldn't arrive till later we left our hand luggage and went for a wander.

3:45 we had to be in our muster stations - ours was deck 4 Y6 in the Eclipse Theatre for lifeboat drill (without life jackets, ours are under our big bed) then on deck as we sailed out of Southampton.

Eventually returned to 'cabin' and re-united with our 3 cases: red one, foine, smaller brown one has a faulty fasten, other brown one's lining left residue on top and bottom clothes so both to be scrapped! Changed into smart casual outfits for dinner. We were on 6pm sitting, table 216 D3 with Ann and Victor from Whitehaven. Met our waiters Tammy and Felix.

To 9pm show, good, especially Ukraine trio, 2 female violnist and a male big celloist.

Hardly any sleep again. 6am ship swaying!

Monday 23rd September

At Sea

Up to Oceanview Restaurant for buffet breakfast. I had fruit salad and yoghurt and a round of brown bread toast plus spreads and coffee. Still suffering from 'mal de mer' so after we returned to cabin I lay down and stayed in darkness when Brian attended a talk on the excursions. After 12 we explored a little more, then Brian ate lunch and I just drank milk in Oceanview. Explored swimming pool areas, i.e. solarium, indoor one with waves. Later noticed it had been emptied and was closed. Wandered in and out of shops - mostly expensive jewellery and leather bags. Bought 2 postcards of Eclipse. Not able to buy a watch battery. Looked round art exhibition, a good mixture.

4:30 to Trivia general knowledge quiz - didn't do too well, 5/15. Winners got 13! Then back to get ready for dinner - I felt worse in our room, but better in the restaurant. I chose fruit, soup, fish and finished with creme brule and drank water.

To 8:30 show - Lindsey Hamilton an excellent singer accompanied by celebrity 7 men orchestra. A great evening.

Explored some more - library.

Took piriton and out straight away till 8:30am. Brian had a poor night with indigestion and was sick.

Tuesday 24th September

At Sea

11:15am To Sky Lounge D14 for Trivia General Knowledge Quiz, guests v officers - a lot of fun. Guests won 13-9.

Explored select section of the ship where non-inclusive restaurants are. I sat at high (closed) bar to write this journal. Brian played grand piano - then, after 20 minutes, was told he was not alllowed to!

Fine art and sculpture on display here.

2pm to Celebrity Central for illustrated talk on other European cruises:- Northern Europe, especially Scandinavia and Russia, South Europe, especially Italy and Greece.

Back to our stateroom for rest, reading and showers, and to dress up for the first Formal Dress evening. Bri looked good in his black lounge suit, white shirt and black bow tie. I wore my black velvet skirt - long 0 and new white lacy glittery top. Had photos taken and I chose duck for dinner, but I left it, too chewy. Waiting staff were very concerned and offered me something else, but I'd shared Bri's salmon so said no. Arranged Bri's birthday treat for 10am. Ann's birthday so cake to share.

8:30pm in theatre - Captain's EReception with champagne.

Evening show called Edge, brilliant dancing, singing, acrobatics non-stop. Everybody around looked fab. On to Quasar Night Club to listen to ABBA music. Arranged 8am wake up call.

25th September
Brian's 80th Birthday

We both had disturbed night.

Wake-up call at 7am!! Bri opened his 12+ cards and displayed them. Went up to Oceanview for freshly squeezed orange juice. Could see North African mountains. Down to DJ Moonlight Sonata for breakfast - actually had cooked food! To Excursions Deck for shuttle bus tickets. Back to D3 and met Alexandros for Bri's treat - a tour of the wine tower which holds 2500 bottles of beer (elsewhere on the ship is a store that holds twenty times that, including beers!). Fascinating tower with steps inside, had different wines explained, some costing 2 to 3 hundred dollars each.

The wine tower

Back to stateroom to collect passports and euros for going ashore. 1pm ship docked at Malaga. Allowed off after 1:30 and shuttle to end of port area.

Walked to our usual plaza in front of the cathedral for cafe con leche - at last, a good cup of coffee! To Calle Larios, bought stamp from Tobacos. Tapas lunch with wine. Posted Eclipse cards to grandchildren and to Joan, Bri's cousin. Walked round narrow streets, sat in Alemeda reading for a while then shuttle back to ship. Before negotiating long winding ramp, greeted with welcome fruit punch and ice cold towel. To 7152 to relax, then change for dinner.

At the end of the meal Tammy, the waiter, bought Bri's birthday cake and we sang to him.

With fellow table guests on Brian's birthday

To theatre, ordered cocktails - my pinacolada delicious. Bri not keen on his 'rusty nail' Drambuie and whisky. Hypnotist's show - we weren't very impressed. Up to see Sunset Bar on Lawn Deck 15. Party on D12 but we went to bed.

Thursday 26th September

At Sea

12 noon we went to a Faberge Talk. Karl Faberge made jewellery - we were shown a gent's watch for £5,500. One Easter he decided to make his wife something different to cheer her up so he made his first egg. She loved it so he made her one each Easter. When the Russian Revolution happened they were all lost. He left a daughter but this creativity seemed to have missed a generation. However, her son inherited it and he was a wood turner. When he was persuaded to make a Faberge egg he made one in beauiful polished wood which was solid. Then he eventually produced eggs like his grandfather's. Several of these were on display varying in price from £2,500 to £35,000. They are beautifully coloured and decorated, coming apart to reveal treasures, e.g. a gold church, a gold candelabra, and a painted flower arrangement.

After lunch we went to a talk (with sangria) about other cruises, then reading up on solstice deck.

The evening's show was Greg Scott, an excellent violinist.

We went into Qasar for a while to listen to karaoke.

Friday 27th September

Nice and Eze Tour

Up on D14 reading till 12 noon, on ship-to-shore tender at Villefranche. On coach with guide Dominique and driver Antoine. Panoramic tour of newer Nice, then guided walk via flower and general market to old Nice, then some free time. Brian went to the farmacie for Gaviscon individual powerders, then to Tobac for stamps. We bought ice creams then on to bus - after passing police security people and camermen outside a hotel where Mr Sarkozy was dining. Coach drove along the coast to Eze, a pleasant drive.

Ezes is a pretty village, built on a hillside so up steep, narrow streets with steps - a walkway really. Eze has 2 hotels, specialist shops, a cafe and vehicles in a big carpark at the bottom before the climb.

Back to Villefranche and tender to the ship after a lovely day in sunshine. 5:30pm when we were back in our stateroom, so a quick wash and change for dinner.

After dinner in Celebrity Central to hear about Rome.

Tonight's show was a comedienne called Hilary O'Nielle, also a vocalist. She was good.

We booked a 7am wake-up call for the next morning.

Posted card to Jon in Eze.

Taken on 27th September 2013

Saturday 28th September

Rome Panoramic Tour

7am wake-up call, ready then to Oceanview for breakfast. Sunny and hot in Rome.

9:15 coach, not much leg room. Good road from Citivavecchia port to Rome. Drove underground to coach station. Dominique led us - holding high a 26 sign for us to follow. Quite a walk on cobbles, an escalator and flight of steps to street level and much traffic into side street (our meeting place later) then she left us for 3/4 hour free time. It took 1/4 hour to queue for the Ladies!

Stood in Saint Peter's Square and took photographs. Crowds of people - very long queues to enter the Basilica. Went for a coffee then time to meet up.

Panoramic Tour verty good, saw so much - Spanish Steps, Roman remains, palaces, churches, the Forum and Coliseum.

Arrived back at 2:45pm, so after dropping off our bags in our room, went up for late lunch as feeling hungry for first time on board.

Wrote card to Beryl but not able to post it where we were.

Stayed on D14 reading till 5pm.

Good dinner then to show - comedian Jeff Stevenson. He was very funny.

Then up to D15 to watch the glass blowing - amazing stuff. Had blankets as windy out in open air.

Sunday 29th September

Livorno

Docked at Livorno for Pisa and Florence.

Weatherwise awful - heavy rain and cooler. Fortunately we hadn't booked a tour though we had intended visiting the port town. Instead stayed on board and lay on sunbeds in solarium, reading by indoor pool. I had an enjoyable swim (6 lengths). Brian didn't come in as he was still putting drops in his ears. He stayed there when I returned to cabin for shower to wash and set hair. Bri replied to Colin's text.

After lunch we played table tennis. I felt very sorry for those people who'd been on trips - they'd got very wet.

Evening show was OK - celebrity pianist who was also a vocalist but his performance was a bit too "camp" for me. I must say for a man his age, he was agile and very light on his feet.

Liberty Eclipse set sail at 9pm.

Monday 30th September

Genoa

7am ship docked in Genoa, a very big city. Beautiful hot sunny day. We walked into city. Came across market stalls and bought nick nacks for granddaughters and Beth, a purse for me (small beaded one) and fridge magnet for Brian. Then stopped for coffee. Walked on until we reached the cathedral, attractive black and white marble facade. Wore Turkish "scarf" over shoulders and arms (turquoise with butterflies) to go inside – impressive.

Brian in Genoa

Then asked a policeman where I could post a card - he didn't know! A man directed us to post office so sent Beryl's card.

Genoa Cathedral

Walked to main square, Piazza Ferrari, with a splendid central fountain feature. Briefly rested in a park on long meandering walk to Columbus Square - even then we didn't find his house! On the way back walked through a long tunnel with much traffic - Galleria Giuseppe Garibaldi. Bought, wrote and posted card to Beth.

Back to ship for lunch. Read, then Trivia Quiz. Showers and formal dress for dinner. Excellent 'Eclipse' Show, thrilling acrobats etc. 9:15 captain and officers mingling, spoke briefly to Captain, long chat with Sue Denning, cruise director - she comes from Lancashire and has visited Thurnham Hall.

Thursday 1st October

At Sea

In spite of a good night's sleep, Midnight to 7am, felt tired all day.

Hot, sunny but windy day - too windy for us to sit outside and read. Anyway, by 9am most sunbeds were occupied! Bri took kindle to I Lounge D6, to be charged. 10:30 attended lecture on different Roman house styles. History specialist disappointing as she read notes all the time and had monotonous voice. Also cold with air conditioning on (Celebrity Central D4) so off for coffee. Had early lunch after reading for a while. 1pm informative talk on how the ship moves; full room for this, given by senior engineers - about engines, propulsion, fuel consumption and stabilizers etc. Quite technical but interesting.

Played table tennis (3rd time). Attended talk and video on the Galapagos Islands tour; 7 days, small Celebrity ship, only 96 people, no formal evenings.

More reading then ready for dinner, after which looking at bracelets for sale.

Another brilliant show - last night's tightrope walker/acrobat was magician tonight - very talented young man. Went out on top deck briefly for view. Then watched dancing, "Groove" on 4. Up and down in lift for better view as crowds everywhere.

To room by 10:30, reading till 12:20

Disturbed night, up twice hot and blocked ????

Wednesday 2nd October
Gibraltar

Up late for breakfast at 9am. It had rained overnight. Our safe would not lock so Bri waited in for Security to come and put it right. Meanwhile I came to sit here in Team Earth to write up this journal.

We had early lunch. Eclipse docked at Gibraltar at 1pm. Temperature was 81 degrees Fahrenheit, the hottest day of the cruise. We went in an 8 seater taxi for guided tour - in St. Michael's Cave and also Siege Tunnels. Here I stood on raised steped by cannon then stepped backwards missing step and fell with a bang - all shook up but not really hurt! Tour ended at one end of Main Street. I got £50 cash from Nat West hole-in-the-wall but it was in Gibraltar pounds, which are not accepted in the UK.. In Marks and Sparks bought a bra and was able to change notes to UK pounds. Bought 2 postcards and stamps and wrote cards to Christine and Carol while drinking coffee then posted them. Brian bought himself a smart Gibraltar hat - bluey green.

Evening show was Philip Browne, very talented vocalist.

Clocks went back 1 hour at Midnight.

Gibraltar, with apes

The Rock of Gibraltar

The Moorish Castle, Gibraltar

Grand Casemate Gates, Gibraltar

Thursday 3rd October

Lisbon

Up early for breakfast then on Deck 14's steps, to watch ship sail up the River Tagus and especially to pass under September Bridge with less than a metre's clearance - awesome experience. We joined a queue for an open-topped 'bus tour but a long queue and shortage of buses (and no seats when they did pull up) so we decided to explore on our own. We walked through Old Lisbon, hilly and cobbled roads with trams. We visited big church, San Fe (???), which had beautiful rose windows, then stopped for a coffee and from there spied a lift to the Castle area.

Lisbon, Portugal

Up in it and still had some climbing to do to reach the Castle entrance. We didn't go in but explored the surrounding area - little shops and a cafe where we ate the delicious Portuguese custard delicacy and had another coffee, all for 4 Euros. We walked back following steep steps. En route Bri bought 2 bottles of port and 1 of wine.

Back at the Eclipse, Bri had to hand in the bottles. We went up to Oceanview for delicious bread and butter pudding lunch. Then reading on D12.

A good show again, Clair Maldin pianist and singer. Watched officers paired with guests doing dance-offs - very funny performances!

Ship rolling a bit so took an anti-sea sickness tablet.

Friday 4th October
At Sea

I slept very well, Brian also. At 8:50am we were awakened by Lazaro (our stateroom attendant)! Up to Oceanview for porridge. From 10am to 1pm in Moonlight Sonata, brunch was being served. There was a beautiful display of all sorts of food, interspersed with fantastic ice sculptures - also two chocolate fountains, one white and one brown, with marsh mallows and pieces of fruit to dip in. We went to look at 10:40 then Brian went to a history lecture on the Mary Rose and Titanic. I wen to the Aqua Beauty and Health Centre to attend a seminar on "How to get a flat tummy"! We learnt that coffee, iced water after a meal, lipstick, mascara and sun lotion, also sweeterners are bad for us. Exercise, correct diet (especially 5 fruit and veg daily) and detoxifaction are what will help to flatten our tums!

Eventually met up with Bri at the Brunch - I loved the chocolate-dipped marshmallows.

Both to a talk by an officer involved in the ship's recycling - interesting. Then to hear the Staff Captain's talk on 'Where the Sexton meets the Stars"

Then we took part in another Trivia quiz on Elvis songs but we weren't very good. We read until 3:30 UK time then went to tea.

Tonight was the 3rd and last formal dress evening. We had a "portrait" photograph taken, a full-length one.

Maureen's portrait picture

The evening show was excellent, called "Ovations" by the same dance group who did "Edge" and "Eclipse". It was non-stop from one routine to the next, an energetic and enjoyable performance.

Saturday 5th October

At Sea

After breakfast we went to see all our photos - 3 from the first formal evening, one from the 2nd and the portrait from the 3rd. The first 4 were 22.95 dollars each and the portrait 29.95. Unfortunately, a strap was hanging out of my white lacy top so we rejected the portrait and chose one from the 1st set. Then we looked round the jewellery sale but everything was still too expensive. So I went to Team Earth to write up my journal. Brian met me there and at 12 o'clock we went to Celebrity Central, D4, to see the documentary on the building of the Celebrity Reflections which was very interesting, and lasted 1 and a half hours.

At 3pm we watched Officers versus Guests table tennis tournament. Brian entered and played well but his partner didn't seem to know the rules so they lost to the officers.

Brian playing table tennis

Show times brought forward to 7pm and 9pm so as it was it was always nearer 7:30 before we finished dining it meant we would go to the 9pm one. We returned to our room, changed into tomorrow's clothes and then were able to finish packing our 3 cases, labelled them, and put outside our door. They had to be there by 11pm and it was only 8:30 so a good job done!

In the evening's show to entertain us was Jeff Stevenson and again he was very funny, Peng Fei Su who did a few magic tricks and Claire Maidin playing the piano and singing.

Arranged for early morning call for 7am. To bed earlier than usual. Our cases were taken overnight.

Sunday 6th October
End of Cruise

Brian was awake at 6:30am so we didn't need the early morning call. Up for early breakfast and this time we had porridge and a cooked meal.

We collected our hand luggage from our stateroom and sat in Qasar lounge reading until our number was called (36 on our luggage labels) so we followed the crowd to the gangway and used our ship passcard for the last time.

In the terminal we found our 3 big cases easily under the 36 sign and we then found the car and filled the boot, and began our journey home.

Brian and Maureen on the Celebrity Eclipse

Ice sculptures and goodies aboard ship

Seeking the Northern Lights

February 2014

Some time after returning from our cruise around the Western Mediterranean, Maureen began to experience quite severe discomfort in her lower back region. This she initially ascribed to poor posture, but eventually she had to visit the doctor. She was sent to Hereford hospital for tests, and whilst awaiting results an offer came, via Diamond Resorts timeshares, to join a fly/cruise to the northern reaches of Norway, to "chase the Northern Lights". It being a significant omission in our experiences, we quickly accepted, and the process of preparing to join the party got under way.

We were advised that in February the weather in and around Norway would be much colder than in the U.K. so we went shopping for cold-weather underwear and headgear. Travel arrangements were being made by the specialist arm of DRL, and all we had to do was to pay for them, including a pre-flight hotel overnight stop at Manchester airport. Anticipation was heightened as departure time drew nearer, but this was cast into serious doubt due to Maureen's worsening condition. We naturally advised Diamond Resorts, who kindly agreed to refund the cost of the holiday if necessary. But Maureen held on, this being one of her long-held "bucket wishes", and eventually we agreed to travel, if we could, to meet the party at the hotel.

The night before leaving home was indeed problematical. Maureen's pain was such that I had to call on the out-of-hours doctor late that night. He gave Maureen pain relief and advised us not to travel, but left the decision to her. The following morning she "said" she felt better, so we eventually loaded the car and set off for Manchester, where we met up at the Hilton as arranged with the rest of the party. Depositing Maureen at the front door I quickly parked the car at the rear of the hotel, then joined her in the foyer. The organisers there were most surprised, though very pleased, to see us, and after our evening meal we settled down to talk, and eventually to sleep.

The Kong Harald

Next morning it was a question of....do we---or don't we? Maureen insisted that we go, so we did, joining the others on the shuttle to the nearby airport terminal. It didn't seem too long before we were airborne and winging our way towards Tromso, on the north-west coast of Norway. At the airport, taxis were waiting to carry us under and through the tunnel into the town, unloading us at the quayside where our ship, the Kong Harald of the Hurtigruten line, was awaiting us. We were, at last, on our way to see the lights.

Our accommodation on the ship was quite basic, but adequate, and the other areas, together with the standard of the food, was good. Wine was provided at our evening meal, though Maureen did cause some consternation when she asked instead for a glass of milk. This had never been requested before and it was only after some delay that it was made available.

Maureen aboard the Kong Harald

Brian aboard the Kong Harald

Maureen ashore in Norway

Dockside in Norway

We anchored overnight before starting off early again, coasting past little dolls houses lining the shore, and then out into the fiord, where the scenery of high snow-covered cliffs and rolling hills was quite majestic. At our next stop we disembarked and walked through the slushy snow…….it was not as cold as we had been lead to believe it might be. We called in at a coffee shop, where the proprietor told us tales of life under the German occupation during WW2, and of the destruction they had caused while withdrawing. That was why most buildings were new, and the houses were like freshly-painted dolls houses. We carried on along the road to the new Arctic Cathedral, and viewed from the cemetery opposite. The design of the cathedral is wedge-shaped, much in keeping with the modernistic appearance of other buildings of note in the town. That evening, having said our farewells to Kong Harald, we were to be bussed out across the bridge to our final overnight stop at the Radisson Blu hotel.

The Arctic Cathedral, Tromso

Inside the cathedral at Tromso

Next day there were to be various options, like a husky sledge ride, or a night in an ice hotel, but we had chosen to take the ski-lift to its viewpoint above the town. Here, while many congregated on the outside platform, Maureen settled herself by the fireside, and I prowled around taking snapshots of the town below. Back at street level we awaited our transport which would return us to our hotel for a rest and a final meal before once more boarding the coach after midnight to seek out the "lights". We drove for over an hour to get away from the effect of artificial lighting in the areas we went through, but eventually stopped for refreshment. I got off the coach and followed a group around the bend and…..there they were, the LIGHTS.

The Northern Lights

Not strong at first, but as we watched they became brighter and more colourful. I returned to Maureen, still in the coach, and with some assistance from the driver got her in a position such that she too could see the spectacle. So, for us, the end had been achieved…..and given us something to remember for the rest of our days, a period which was to prove too short for Maureen, who passed away a short two months later, having been diagnosed with aggressive pancreatic cancer.

THE END

Maureen

Second Helpings of Turkey

November 2015

Traditionally, Christmas time is "turkey time", but I have already had mine…twice this year. In November I returned to that fascinating land of history and exoticism, with its archeological remains, whirling dervishes, fairy castles and magic carpets (not that I found one of those). We arrived at Istanbul Sabiha Gokcen airport on the European side, and gazed across the Bosphorus to Asia; Istanbul is the only capital in the world with a foot in two continents. Once known as Chalcedon, it later morphed into Byzantium before the Roman emperor Constantine named it first Nova Roma (can you guess?) built a defensive wall, a great palace, baths, forums and several Christian churches, later renaming it Constantinople. In 1453 the Turks, a people from the north, invaded the city; their sultan Mehmet turned the church of St. Sophia into a mosque, and so began the rise of Islam in Turkey.

The Hagia Sophia mosque, Istanbul

In modern times Turkey sided with Germany (who they saw as a possible trading partner) during World War One, but by the war's end Turkey had lost all its mid-eastern possessions. But Mustapha Kemel, the Turkish commander at Gallipoli, abolished the sultanate and became the obvious choice as president of the new republic in 1923. He was later honoured with the title of Ataturk, father of the nation, and the country abounds with statues and pictures of him. And it was he, realising how hard it was to defend Istanbul (the capital's new name) who transferred to seat of government to Ankara in the centre of the country.

Juice seller, Istanbul

Why, you may ask, did I return to Turkey this time? An opportunity arose, as part of a guided coach tour, to visit centres of historical and architectural antiquity, whilst luxuriating in 5-star hotels and partaking of high-quality Turkish and European cuisine. We flew by Freebird (the Turkish Airline's charter arm) from Birmingham, arriving late evening and being whisked along busy and brightly-lit roads to our hotel. Turkey is a peaceful and prosperous Muslim country, and an ideal destination for Western tourists. Its climate in our wintertime is mild and pleasant, and in order to promote tourism the government provides financial support in an otherwise dead season to hotels, and other tourist-related activities. And, although not yet a member of the European Union, it accepts the euro alongside the Turkish lira, and most establishments accept credit cards.

The Istanbul market

Next day we returned to Istanbul and de-bussed in the Old City in Sultan Ahmed square, previously site of the Roman Hippodrome. We passed by the German fountain and the Egyptian obelisk before walking into the complex housing the Blue Mosque, with its six minarets, and decorated internally with 20,000 blue ceramic tiles. We inspected the Topkapi Palace, once home to the Ottoman sultanate, before coming to the Hagia Sophia mosque, now a museum. In addition to four minarets, it boasts a most impressive interior, with its great cupola and surrounding galleries in which the women used to pray. We took lunch on the terrace café, with views up the Bosphorus and along the Golden Horn towards the Black Sea. Later, we took a river trip to and under those bridges which join Europe to Asia. That evening saw us visiting the nearby bazaar, with its myriad spices, confectionery, jewellery and, unusually, gaily-plumaged cage-birds of many kinds.

View up the Bosphorus

To cross into Asia one can either drive over the bridges, or through the new road tunnel or, as we did next morning, drive down past the battle areas of the Gallipoli peninsular to the ferry at Canakkele. In Asia we made for the city of Troy, devastated in the 12th century by a series of earthquakes. The city, once the scene of the 10-year Trojan war, was also the setting for Homer's Iliad, and had been rediscovered and excavated by the German archaeologist Heinrich Schliemann. Outside the city is a huge reproduction wooden horse, into which tourists- as we did – may climb. We had time to tour the city's remains before heading to our hotel at Ayvalik and the enticing buffet laid on.

A modern reimagining of the wooden horse of Troy

Sardis was once the capital of the Lydian kingdom and seat of the fabulously-rich King Croesus. Here we explored the Temple of Artemis, Roman synagogue and baths/gymnasium complex, all now in ruins, before moving on to our hotel at Denzili. Next morning we came to the recently-excavated city of Laodicea, walking the 900-metre long Syrian road, and sitting in two great theatre complexes. Roman politics demanded that, when a Parliament was convened, the whole town was involved, and so one of the arenas had to be large enough to accommodate the whole population of the town. Also recently unearthed is one of the world's oldest churches, and the symphean fountains.

Sardis today

Later we journeyed through the Taurus mountains to the white-clad mountain at Pamukkele, also home to the city of Hierapolis (which was not on our itinerary this time). Hot springs depositing calcium carbonate cascade over the terraces, resulting in the white coating. On a visit some years earlier we were permitted to walk on and even bathe in these springs but, now that it is a World Heritage site, this has been forbidden. On the outskirts of Antalya we stopped to gaze at a cliff-based waterfall, and the huge face beside it carved from the rock, before proceeding to our hotel outside the city.

Next morning we were taken to the magnificent Roman arena at Aspendos, built in 155 A.D. and now the oldest and best-preserved of its kind in Turkey. At its height it was capable of seating over 7,000 spectators to watch the plays and the games, and to listen to Roman orators. Aspendos was once a thriving centre of trade, and even had its own coinage around 1500

B.C. Whilst the Eurymedon river remained navigable the city derived great wealth from trade in oils, salt and wool, but its silting-up heralded its decline into obscurity The river is crossed by the Roman bridge, destroyed by the earthquake of May 363 A.D. (which also severely damaged the theatre) and rebuilt in a zig-zag formation. Nearby too is a now-ruined Roman aqueduct, constructed in the early 2nd century to bring water to the city.

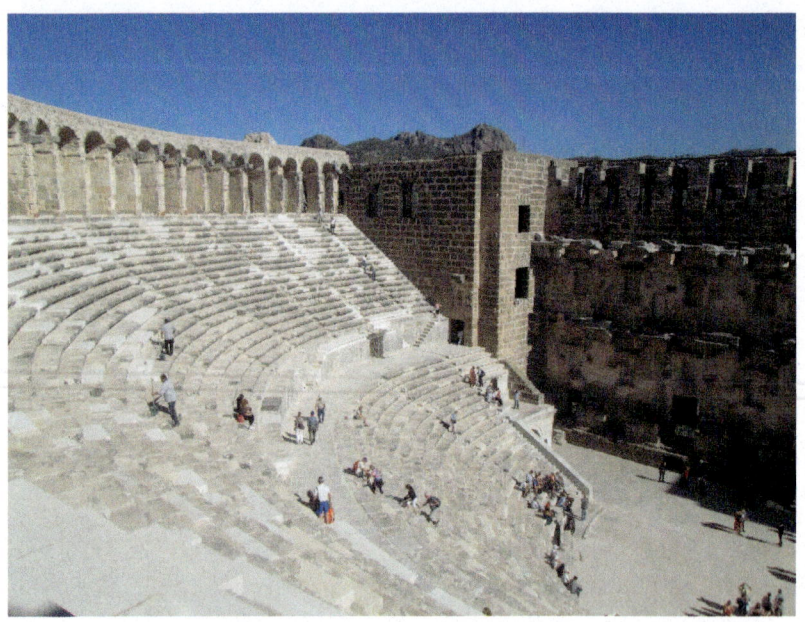

Roman arena at Aspendos

The afternoon found us first gazing in awe at the Duden Falls outside the city, where the river drops sheer into the sea. Then on to the old part of Antalya, around and above the harbour. Here can be seen a statute of Ataturk, the 'father' of modern Turkey. A short walk further on is Hadrian's Gate, set in the city wall. All around this area are stalls and shops selling typical Turkish merchandise; if you don't like the price, just haggle. We ended up in a café just across the tram-tracks, where one of our party was presented by the owner with a birthday cake, amidst much celebration.

The Duden Waterfalls

During our time in Turkey we also took in visits to a leather factory, a jewellery establishment and a carpet manufactory, where a few women ably demonstrated the art of carpet-weaving, most nowadays working from home. These carpets were of many sizes and designs, and at the end we understood just why some of them sold for very high prices. The opportunity to buy at each of the sites was taken up by some members of the party….but not by me!

So to our final morning. We transferred to the airport, the third largest in Europe behind London and Paris, and eventually boarded our Freebird flight back to Birmingham. The end of a great week's sightseeing in a truly fabulous country. What did I learn? Well, most importantly, that empires, kings and even their monuments do not live for ever, many disappearing completely from history. And that this world is a most amazing place, with many scenes and sights still to be discovered. I hope that I shall be able to continue to so do for some time to come.

Brian G. Davies

*Istanbul airport is known (to some) as Sabiha Gokcen

Brian in Turkey

A Glimpse of Heaven
– in North-West Devon

March 2016

A recent opportunity saw me driving down from mid-Wales, via the notorious Newport tunnel on theM4, and the Severn Bridge crossing, and into Devon, where I would be staying for the next week. This location was so near to the Cornish west coast that Bude was only a short drive away. However, my inclinations led me further north, first to the small 'village' of Clovelly, and then subsequently to the one-time port of Hartland. This area is well-known for its connections with cream teas, smuggling and shipwrecks, and it was these last two that I wanted to explore in more detail.

First then to Clovelly, on the north coast on a sunny though chilly March day. The last time I had visited was with family in the summer of 1991, when there were hordes of visitors to contend with. This time it was relatively deserted so, having paid my £7 parking and entry fee at the Visitor Centre I began the descent, calling first at Mount Pleasant where there is a war memorial and spectacular views over the harbour. A short walk further on brings you to Clovelly Court, with its gardens and the 15th C. parish church of All Saints. And then begins the descent in earnest…on a cobbled roadway which leads down the cleft in the cliffs, and is lined with over 70 listed buildings….a veritable architectural treasure store.

Clovelly has been privately owned by only three families since the 13th C. It also boasts two public houses, two hotels and the erstwhile home for a while of the author Charles

Kingsley....remember the Water Babies, and Westward Ho, both inspired by his time in the village.

Car traffic is banned in the village, and provisions and other items have to be dragged up/down the road by sledge, either manually or with the help of donkeys, who are also employed in giving children rides in summer-time. Near to Kingsley's house is the small chapel of St. Peter, a daughter church of the parish church since 1948 and in earlier times used as a schoolroom for evacuees from London, Bristol and Plymouth. Prominently displayed in the church are three quite recent murals depicting the angels Gabrielle and Raphael, and the message they brought to all men through the Lamb of God.

Clovelly harbour and mole

Eventually one comes down to the harbour, where creels are still stacked on the breakwater, and boats sit on the sea awaiting their next call to set sail. West of the harbour is the lifeboat station; due to piracy and smuggling being rife in the 19th C Clovelly has since 1860 had its own lifeboat. Then, after a lunchtime visit to the nearby Lion Hotel we look for the expected transport back to the Visitor Centre but, it being out of season at present, it's not running, so to walk back is the only option. Oh, well… Best foot forward then! But a great visit, which I can highly recommend.

Another day saw us travel around Hartland Point and down the coast a bit to Hartland Quay, once a thriving port but nowadays reduced to Club and tourist activity only. A lookalike to the one at Clovelly, Hartland Quay was built at the end of the 16th C to facilitate the shipping out of coal, lime and slate, and the bringing in of grain and other material. At the quayside there was a shop which stocked building and domestic items needed by the householders. There was also a malthouse for the brewing of beer, and a pub, next to which was a bank -Hoskins & Son - issuing its own currency. However, all this ceased when the railway came to Barnstaple and maintenance of the pier stopped. By 1896 most of it had been destroyed by storms and a way of life disappeared. Nowadays most of the buildings have been converted into a hotel.

The majority of ships calling at Hartland Quay were quite small – only up to 150ft long, but the area became notorious for the wrecks of much larger ships driven, or even lured, aground and onto the razor-sharp rocks. A peaceful and scenic setting today, the area has seen more than its fair share of tragedy, with ships such as the SS Uppingham being wrecked in 1890 with the loss of many lives. Its boiler can still be seen today on the rocks at low tide.

Hartland Quay – the beach

Hartland Quay – the main street

Italy – Top to Toe

2016

I had been to Venice some years earlier with my late wife, and had been mesmerised by its superficial beauty and the many canals, but when I recently saw it was to be the start of a two-week coach trip along the length of Italy's western coast I had to make a booking. And I was not disappointed….Venice, on Italy's Adriatic coast, was an ideal starting point. We flew by British Airways from Gatwick to the airport outside Venice and transferred that evening to our hotel at Lido de Jesolo. This was to be the first of four 4* hotels we would use, and for most of us these proved good accommodation. My only concern…for those of us who were single the rooms allotted to us were rather small and skimpy, but nevertheless, food on a half-board basis was good and the locations were well-chosen.

Rialto Bridge, Venice

The next morning we were coached to the ferry for the crossing to the pier adjacent to St. Mark's Square. We were soon joined by our local guide, who took us on a walk around and across some of the multitudinous canals on which the city is built. The daily business was in evidence, with boats carrying all kinds of cargo being piloted skilfully around corners, up narrow waterways and under bridges, and gondoliers in their traditional costume and black-painted gondolas punting tourists from one point of interest to another. A major such point is the Rialto Bridge, sadly now hiding beneath a covering whilst maintenance work is carried out. However, our subsequent free time allowed us to push our way along its length, where shops selling a variety of merchandise are in evidence, and nearby artists and ice-cream vendors are always on the look-out for a discerning traveller.

Saint Mark's Square, Venice

Having seen some of the many palaces which abound in the city, the most well-known being the Doge's Palace with its 'Bridge of Sighs' to the adjacent prison, I took a "vaparetto" (water-bus) along the Grand Canal returned to St. Mark's Square, and joined a small and fast-moving queue to enter the Cathedral. Here, two twisted columns behind the altar are said to have formed part of Solomon's temple, whilst the four bronze horses above the basilica's façade came from Constantinople. The external bell-tower is a copy of the one which collapsed in 1902. On leaving the building I had to step through some water, and discovered that the incoming tide had forced its way up through a grating. This is a not unusual occurrence, and only the week before had in fact given rise to a quite considerable flooding of the square. It was now almost time to return to our departure point…where was it? After almost a half-hour without any of my party appearing I decided to walk along to the pier, and was, thankfully, met by our tour manager, who returned with me to the correct boat. This was to be only the first of four occasions when I found myself "lost"…not a happy experience, I assure you.

Church of San Petronio, Bologna

Next morning we joined the nearby motorway and set off towards our next night's stop. En route we passed by Padua, and stopped for a few hours in the 'Red City' of Bologna, so called because of the eye-catching stone which features greatly in the architecture of this medieval city. Also of note here are the many covered colonnades, which allow shoppers to wander the streets in the rain without getting wet. As it was raining on our visit here we no doubt made good use of these. We had some hours of free time to occupy, so I wandered amongst the ancient buildings, and taking many photographs. On the edge of the Piazza Maggiore is the imposing church of San Petronio, outside of which was stationed a 'caribinieri, presumably in case of terrorist attack. Soon I had wandered away from the tourist sights and, once again, was lost, and had to ask my way back of a helpful but non-English-speaking Italian 'signor'.

Between us, he got the gist of my query, and soon I was sitting at a pavement café having a well-earned lunch. The city is well-known for its bolognaise sauce, and for 'granita', a kind of frozen black coffee with whipped cream. Rejoining my group at the appointed place, we set off for our night's hotel in the town of Montecatini Terme, our base for the next three nights. That evening we experienced our first real storm...thunder and lightning...for which the area is renowned.

Montecatini is a spa town...not that we had much opportunity to make use of the thermal springs there. Next day was a half-day included excursion to Pisa. The weather now was good, and the city was full of tourists all determined to make a day of it, some even attempting (photographically) to push the Leaning Tower back to the vertical. I opted for the Baptistry and having purchased the necessary ticket ascended the 70-odd stairs to the gallery for a birds-eye view. Later I visited the Cathedral (free that day) and then walked around to the Tower, where tourists were queuing for some time before entering.

Time was pressing, however, so I made my way back to the meeting point with our tour manager Armundo, before we all walked back to the coach park for the return to the hotel. The afternoon was "free time" so a number of us walked to the funicular, and were whisked up to the heights above the town…spread out before us it was quite a sight.

The Baptistry at Pisa

The main excursion next day was to Florence, but I had previously "done that", so instead decided to catch the train to Lucca, a walled pre-Roman city further west towards the coast. The weather was glorious, and tourists abounded, some even cycling along the top of the city wall. After walking for quite some time amongst the many interesting buildings, including several churches and the home of the composer Puccini, with his statute reclining in the nearby square, I found myself in the Plaza "Amphitheatre", and took the opportunity, as so many others were doing, of partaking of a café lunch. Eventually I found my way to the bus station and returned to Montecatini, arriving just in time for the rain which had, apparently, been more in evidence for the group visiting Florence that day.

Mediaeval gateway into Lucca (Porta San Gervasio)

So now, off south along the motorway to Orvieto, set high on its rock of tufa The "duomo", or cathedral was well worth a visit to see its richly-decorated chapel, but a service was pending so we did not linger. Instead, a small group of us joined an excursion into the underground city, a labyrinth of caves and tunnels beneath the city. Over the past 3000 years an unbelievable number of these have been dug, including even pigeon "lofts" for a source of food, and wells dug for a water supply. Remembering my "trip" on a previous holiday in a similar setting I welcomed a kind supporting arm to steady me, just in case, and emerged this time without mishap. And so on to Fuiggi, our preferred stop-over for Rome. Bypassing the "Eternal City" in heavy rain we arrived at the Hotel San Giorgio, our home for the next three nights.

Today the main party was visiting Rome but, having also been there several times before, decided instead to do my own thing and, in company with a few like-minded of our party, took the bus up to medieval Fuiggi Alta, the Old Town. For a time we wandered in the sun amongst some interesting buildings, and the very steep interconnecting stairways from street to street, but eventually succumbed to the temptation of coffee and cake of the region, before catching the bus back down the hill (some hardy souls even walked down!). That afternoon, having heard about some wonderful mosaics in a nearby church, I made my way along the main street to the church, but in the rain actually passed it by. Again, an Italian couple had to direct me, but once inside the mosaics were a sight to behold…the whole interior of the building was covered in mosaic, and I had to walk around on the specially-installed wooden walkways. Despite the rain, it was a worth-while visit.

Brian in Fuiggi

Next morning should have been an optional excursion to some pretty hilltop villages of Castelli Romani, where frascati is a locally-produced wine. However, due to lack of numbers this was cancelled and so once again free time was in evidence, so I walked to the south of the town, and spent an hour or so watching one of Italy's pastimes…cycle racing. Actually, the antics of the policemen on duty there were more interesting, but it passed the time. My return to the town centre was by way of the extensive parkland alongside the main road. For me, Fuiggi was a disappointment, and I was glad to get away from it the next morning. Perhaps a guided tour would have changed my opinion?

Rain was still prevalent as we approached Montecassino Abbey, so the impressive sight of it above the town which I had read about was absent. The Abbey had been the target of heavy sustained bombing by the Allies during WW2, and been razed to the ground. It has now been completely reconstructed and faithfully restored – a fantastic effort. Within the Abbey we were able to wander at will, both inside and amongst the heavily-restored buildings. My guidebook of 1980 makes no mention of the Abbey, perhaps presuming it no longer existed then. Inside the church itself were parties of schoolchildren learning, possibly, about its beauty and its history. Outside, in front of a statue of 'Peace' was a "columbine" of doves (dig that!), very apt in the circumstances. As the rain eased we made our way down the coast towards the world-famous ruins of Pompeii outside Naples. Fortunately, this was a guided tour, and we learned a lot about the fate of this town when Mount Vesuvius had erupted in 79 A.D., and buried the entire area - and its inhabitants - under a layer of hot ash. Today, life as it was here 2000 years ago is once again laid bare. A most interesting and instructive visit. Let's hope the next – and overdue – eruption of Vesuvius is not about to happen! And so, on to the Hotel Tirrenia on the Sorrento peninsular.

Pompeii with Vesuvius in the background

Our excursions for the next days having been changed about, those of us who had opted for the trip set off for the Isle of Capri, once the home of Gracie Fields. Leaving harbour we sailed towards the "Blue Isle", its rugged cliffs as we approached taking on the azure hue of the sky. On landing we were bussed up a winding and narrow roadway (the Via Krupp of the manufacturer's fame) to the island's heights …Anacapri… where we met our guide, who took us for a walkabout. We had free time before lunch, so I took the opportunity to join the queue for the single-person chairlift, which took me to the summit of Monte Solara, the island's highest point, with its wonderful views of the area. Then back down for the non-included lunch, before eventually rejoining the bus and wending our way to the hotel.

Amalfi

The following morning dawned bright and sunny, boding well for our excursion along the Amalfi coast. The roads are very twisty and narrow, and almost choked with traffic of all kinds and sizes. Indeed, the coast has special "wardens" who are employed solely to inform traffic of oncoming vehicles, and to bring about some degree of order to what would otherwise be an intolerable traffic jam. That aside, the views of whitewashed villas and small coves a considerable way below us were stupendous. A good job our driver was excellent as he skilfully piloted us up and along the coastal road. We stopped for some time in the town of Amalfi itself, and later visited the Villa Rufolo in Ravello. This is a mix of restored cloisters, ancient walls and beautiful gardens with their panoramic views. An excellent days' outing, and back to the hotel in Sorrento. Here I had come across a lovely "Bechstein" baby grand piano, at which I was able to indulge myself that evening, and being surprised at the extent and appreciation of an impromptu audience.

Our holiday was now drawing to an end, so we were en route to Sicily, our longest road trip, so we were glad to see the port of Reggio Di Calabria coming into view. A short delay, and we were boarding the ferry for our final leg, across the Straits of Messina and down the road to Taormina and our final hotel for the next three nights. Next morning was an included excursion to the picturesque town, perched high on a sheer cliff across the bay. We were invited to sample Granita, the Sicilian iced drink, and Canoli, a local sweet pastry, before exploring at our own pace the fine historic centre and pretty gardens, and doing some last-minute shopping. Back at the hotel, some of the party took advantage of the sunshine and increased heat to swim in, or sunbathe by, the hotel's fine outdoor pool, and over all brooded the subject of next day's optional excursion, the volcano Mount Etna.

The volcano party departed early, aiming first to take the coach to the lower slopes, and then by funicular to the next stage, before (hopefully) taking taxis to the summit. This latter hope, however, was dashed due to the volcano's sporadic eruptions of gas and larva, and the presence at the summit of vulcanologists working away there. Still, for those who went on the excursion it was an experience not often available, so considered worthwhile. For myself, with others I remained at ground level and walked to the town's harbour, where there were many and varied craft at anchor, including a huge white cruise ship, though too far away to see its name. However, lunch called and proved very adequate, before setting off back on the 30-minute walk to the hotel for our last evening…and the promised champagne before dinner.

Next morning we were up and packed early, despite our plane's departure being mid-afternoon. Then to the airport, with its usual delays and regulations to conform to, before eventually emplaning. Take-off, for me anyway, was quite impressive as I had a good view of Mount Etna, still puffing merrily as we went up and away for our final few hours.

View of Mount Etna from the plane

It had been an excellent, although tiring, trip, but one that I was glad (for more than one reason) to have undertaken. Our group, although mainly of senior ages, jelled well, and when companionship was called for it was available, and that was what I had chiefly gone for…and the photographs, of course. So success, for me, at least. Will anything further come of it? Perhaps, but I will have for the present to wait and see.

Our Scottish Holiday

2016

It was early Spring 2012 and getting on for time to change our car, which has been experiencing gearstick problems for some time. Being a Nissan Primera automatic, it had served us well and even my wife Maureen had been able to drive it competently but, after 10 years, it was showing considerable signs of wear. So, in March we were down in Tredegar visiting our daughter, and to take our three grandchildren for a day out to White Castle on the Welsh/English border.

While waiting for their parents to get the children ready, Maureen and I drove round to the near-by depot of Ron Skinner, from where we had previously bought this Nissan. Now we were looking hopefully for a diesel automatic SUV, with sufficient seats to be able to carry us plus my daughter's family. 'Sorry', the salesman told us, 'we don't have anything like that in stock at the moment.' But I had spotted one which might meet our requirements, though what did I know! The salesman followed us to the far side of the indoor showroom. 'Oh' he said, somewhat shamefacedly. 'A Citroen Gran Picasso 7-seater. This must have come in when I was on leave yesterday.' He then commenced his sales patter, which I had to cut short as we were in danger of losing time. Just confirming that the car was indeed a diesel automatic, and after him showing us the 'dicky' seats in the boot, we confirmed that we would purchase it. 'Don't you want to test-drive it/' he asked. 'No time', I said, 'where do we sign?' Must have been the quickest and easiest sale that he had ever made. We agreed to return in a week's time to collect the car, and he agreed to complete all the usual formalities by then, and off we went to pick up our grand-children. My daughter and son-in-law were amazed at our stupidity, and on reflection they were probably right, but now the die was cast, so off we went for our day out with the children.

****

It was another three years before we were able to put the decision to the test. By that time my wife Maureen had passed away, due to pancreatic cancer, and I was desirous of being able to gather my daughter's family together for a special holiday experience. Having a week's Timeshare in the bank, I had booked a week during August 2016 at the Highland Club at Loch Rannoch towards the west of Scotland.

Arriving at the Highland Club, in the Citroen Gran Picasso

To drive there was the only economic means of travel, and in any case Loch Rannoch was so far off the usual transport routes that a car was a necessity. I had driven down to Swansea the day before and overnighted at my park home at the Riverside Campsite in readiness for an early start. By 8.30 next morning I was collecting the family and getting them and luggage, in some sort of order, into the car. So, with our youngest, Ceridwen, at 8 years old, safely and firmly ensconced in the boot on one of the 'dickie' seats (the other one being the repository for the luggage, food and coats etc), we set off by way of the M4, M5 and M6 for this 'holiday of a lifetime'.

Robin, my son-in-law, had been designated both as co-driver and route-finder but once in Scotland this second task proved a difficulty. Carlisle saw us make a slight diversion to the city's edge for a supermarket stop, before pressing on past Gretna where we picked up the A74(M). This took us past Lockerbie, after which the road wound monotonously through the beautiful rolling scenery of Galloway, Dumfries and South Lanarkshire Eventually, after joining the M73 to bypass Glasgow, we noticed that the city was not, according to my estimation, where it should have been. We had strayed onto the M8 from where, after erroneously crossing the River Clyde, a piece of adroit juggling reversed our direction. After an interesting though at times frustrating drive through and around the city we managed to find our way north-eastwards on the M80 onto the M9 and past Stirling. Perth came....and went, by which time we were all getting tired, although snacks and crisps had staved off, to a large extent, the children's hunger. Not a word of complaint, though, from Ceri, who was cooped up in the back of the car for long periods on end. Well done to her!

Fortunately the weather had stayed fine and, although evening was approaching, it remained quite bright. The A9 bore us ever northwards, and quite soon the lights of Pitlochry came into view. Here we left the main road, and turned west past Loch Tummel into Kinloch Rannoch, where we stopped off to pick up the keys to our apartment. Soon we were turning into the timeshare/hotel complex, had unloaded the car and explored our accommodation. This was a duplex 3-bed unit with a large kitchen/dining/lounge area, and a great glassed-in conservatory running the whole length of the apartment, providing fabulous views over the loch towards the "Faery Mountain", Mount Schiehallion.

View from the conservatory

Bethan and Rob had the big double-bedroom, the two other girls, Imogen (15) and Bryony (13), shared a twin bedroom, and Ceri and myself shared the other (which, I must confess as payer for the holiday, had the best and en-suite bathroom). Outside in the corridor was the communal sauna which naturally appealed to most of the party. So, after a journey of

450 miles and lasting 12 hours we had arrived and were beginning to settle down for the night. And not too soon, for me anyhow. It had been a long day.

++++++++++++++++++++++++++++++++

Our holiday experience did not start well…..at least not from the weather's point of view. Next day it rained off and on, certainly not worth venturing outside, so books, board games and quizzes came into their own. But it was an opportunity to rest and gather ourselves for the rest of the week. Next day we had visitors….Rob's sister Jennie and family, who lived in the Dundee area, came for a few hours. And in the evening the resort had laid on a Highland Experience, which Rob took to with gusto.

Rob's Highland Experience

Even the girls enjoyed dressing up and making safe use of the weapons and protective clothing… claymores, dirks and shields….to hand.

Tuesday morning saw us driving to the Highland Folk Museum at Newtonmore. To get there we headed north on the B287, then joined the A9 through Glen Garry. The girls all took turns at milking a cow (sadly, only a model), then into a 1950's schoolroom typical of the area, visited a Scottish long house and saw some Muscovy ducks parading around an old car chassis.

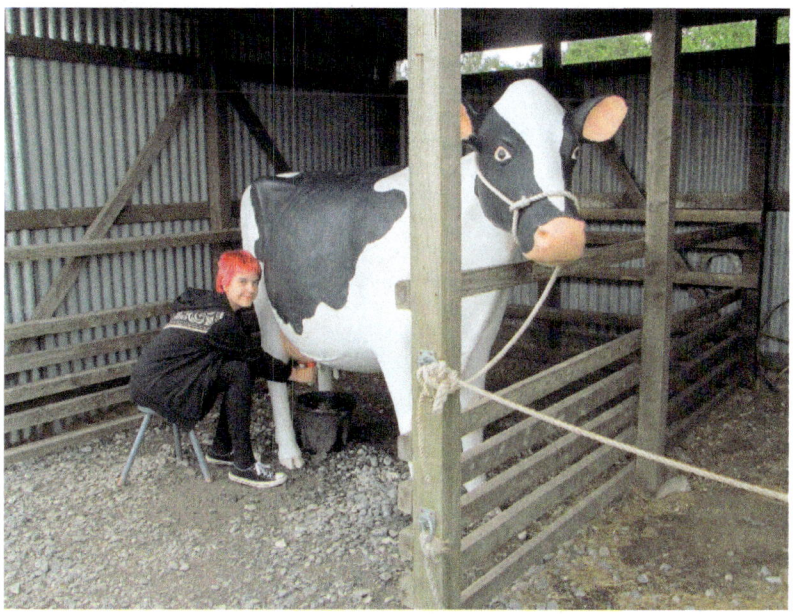

A-milking we will go!

Rob and I found a café to make use of, whilst the 'ladies' all went down to see the recreated 17th century village with its mile-long main street. Too far for me, I'm afraid. Finally, after a visit to the 'munchies' shop, we set off to return to our holiday accommodation.

Next morning dawned bright, and we went down to Reception to meet with Steve, our guide for the day. Boots and anoraks were the order for what was to be quite a demanding trek through the woods on the other side of the lake. We followed Steve in our car, 'til he stopped some way along the single-track road and parked up.

With our poles

Here we were issued with special poles to help us to proceed through the trees and across undulating ground – I admit to needing two of these to help me negotiate the at times quite steep and narrow pathways. At a few points it was necessary to climb over high fences or gates, which Ceri coped with quite nimbly; not so Imogen, who felt that even a 3-bar gate was a replica of Ben Nevis. Even Steve's dog Bramble was able to get over or under such obstacles, with a little help, of course and, on passing the end of the loch, she dashed in for an opportunist swim. At one point we came across the remains of a shepherd's bothy, which we used both for a rest and as a photographic focal point. The clouds occasionally seemed to be at lake level but at least it didn't rain, and we were able at last to cross the last remaining obstacle – a swollen stream –

by way of a stone parapet, and walk the last part of the trek back to the car. Here we said good bye, and thanks, to Steve for his patience with us. Back at the resort that evening, we adults attended a "Whisky Tasting" event which I, not being a lover of this spirit, at some point abandoned it and left Beth and Rob to its delights.

Ceri walking Bramble

Being a member of the Diamond timeshare group I had made arrangements for Ceri and myself to head over to the neighbouring resort of Kenmore which I knew had a swimming pool, so in the morning she and I drove over there for our swim. Afterwards we met up with the rest of the party and headed to the far side of the town, where we visited Loch Tay and The Crannog, a prehistoric hutted site constructed on wooden piles driven into the water. Here we were able to grab a quick snack before trying our hands at wood-turning and breadmaking, and learning of how its early occupants had lived in the area.

The Crannog

Back at Kinloch, we detoured to the left hand side of the lake, where – on the map - was indicated a school. It was here, Rob told us, that he had spent a part of his early days attending this school, which – he said – was not a happy experience. He and another lad had managed to break out one evening, and make their way to Pitlochry before being recaptured and returned next day. The school was now a private house, and well closed off, so unfortunately we were unable to explore further.

The following morning saw us also making our way to Pitlochry. The town was crowded with holiday-makers, and it was difficult to park, but at last we were able to explore the shops, before moving off to see the mysteries of the renowned "fish ladder." The water therein was cloudy and discoloured, and it was explained to us that the correct season for seeing this phenomenon had now passed. The few salmon which remained were small, difficult to make out, and seemingly too tired to expend their energies on 'climbing' the ladder to bypass the dam. On the way back we called at "Queen's View' overlooking Loch Tummel, some think so named in honour of Queen Victoria's visit to it in 1866, but in reality after Queen Isabel, wife of Robert the Bruce. Here, most of us contented ourselves with enjoying this view, though for Ceri it provided a good opportunity for a scramble on the rocks.

Queen's View

And so the day of our departure had dawned. After a quick breakfast cases were finally packed and once again we loaded ourselves into the car. Keys were returned to Reception, a quick call at the village shop, and we were on our way. The B486 took us to Aberfeldy, where we picked up the A826 through Glen Cochill and eventually on to the outskirts of Perth, meeting up here with the M90. After a most pleasant time for all at the Highland Club we were now well on our way, and it was only a matter of retracing our journey north. Once again the supermarket at Carlisle was put to good use, and Rob and I took turns at the wheel for the long haul back to Swansea. If only the Highland Club was nearer, we said, it would be nice to return some day.

Cruising the Mekong River

from Saigon to Siem Reap

My Visit to Vietnam & Cambodia

2018

Having decided to make this long journey a little easier, I travelled from Swansea to Heathrow the day before, then caught the shuttle to my hotel for the night. Next morning, refreshed, I made my way back to Heathrow, to catch Thai Airways midday flight to Bangkok. Here I made an error, trying to make the long walk on my own to the departure lounge. Part-way I gave in, luckily finding a porter with a wheelchair, to finish off this part of the journey. At Bangkok we had to change planes, eventually arriving at Ho Chi Minh City (Saigon) airport around 9.a.m.

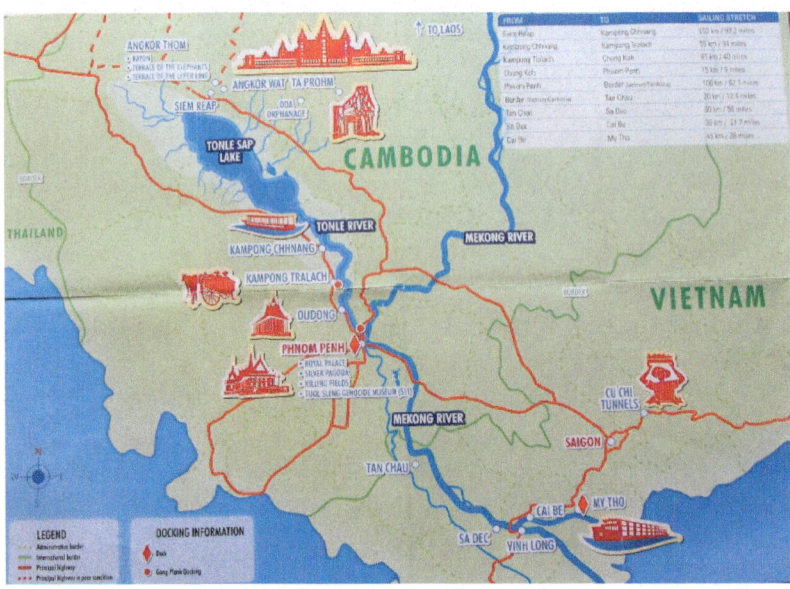

Map of the Mekong as it passes through Vietnam & Cambodia

In the Arrivals Hall a representative of Travelmarvel met us, and transported us to our hotel, The Fusion Suites. On the way we passed several parks and open spaces where students congregated, and encountered the Saigon traffic, comprising chiefly of scooters, motorcycles and bicycles. For the remainder of the day we were at liberty to explore the city, or just to rest up, before our evening meal at KOTO Kumbo restaurant, where we could engage with the local Vietnamese and South East Asian cuisine.

Hidden tunnel entrance

Next day we visited the Cu Chi Tunnel complex, a network constructed by Vietnamese resistance fighters during the First Indochina war against the French. These tunnels were used by the Viet Cong guerrillas in their fight against the Americans as meeting rooms, hospitals, air raid shelters and ammunition factories, also serving as communications and living quarters for fighters and civilians alike. We also saw the many and various mantraps used against their enemies, and a few of our party even ventured underground, one trying to exit through a small opening in the ground initially built for the smaller bodies of the Vietcong soldiers. Again, on returning to our hotel we were at liberty to visit the colourful markets and ancient pagodas, some even venturing out on a shopping or a military jeep tour.

The RV Marguerite

The next morning we were bussed to My Tho port where we joined our ship, the RV Marguerite, our home for us 92 passengers for the next seven nights. We were welcomed with a drink and a short briefing while awaiting lunch. After this our cabins were ready for us, and the ship set sail for Cai Be, our first port of call. Meanwhile, I familiarised myself with the ship's layout, and even met (and talked with) some of my fellow-passengers, many of whom were from Australia. Then came the inevitable safety demonstration and briefing, followed by Captain's Cocktails. Our evening concluded with a gourmet meal, after which we could relax on deck with a (free) drink or two, and watch the surrounding coutryside.

The town of Cai Bai is on the river, and we were able to view the floating markets which chiefly sold fresh fruit and vegetables. Some women were engaged in transporting their wares on small canoe-like boats from one stall to another, and some boats even carried tourists, just like taxis. We then went ashore to visit the town itself, with its French Gothic Cathedral and colonial buildings, and of course its multitude of scooter traffic and put-puts. Back on board we set off for Sa Dec, a city much smaller than Cai Be, but also blessed with many markets of all kinds. Seafood and insect-based "delicacies" (ants and tarantula spiders?) abounded with, sitting alone on a small stool and surrounded by sellers and buyers alike, a young girl, apparently engrossed in her schoolwork, but ready for any customer who might turn up.

After breakfast next morning we donned our lifejackets and boarded small boats, navigating narrow channels and creeks where stilt houses were much in evidence. This not being the rainy season we could see how high up the living quarters were, with long external stairways to reach them.

Once ashore at Tan Chau we visited a silk and rattan mat factory, seeing how silk is processed and exploring the attached shop, where I bought a much-to-be admired silk shirt. Before returning to the ship we toured the village by way of the local unique 'cyclos' known as Xe Loi, (or to us 'rickshaws') and only found in this area of the Mekong. Sitting behind our "driver" I must admit to not seeing much of the terrain, and was glad to return to the ship which, during the afternoon, crossed the border into the kingdom of Cambodia.

We started next morning with a visit to the "Killing Fields" and the Genocide Museum, once a school and now the site of the once notorious Security Prison of Tuoi Sleng. Here, more than 12,000 people were tortured and sent to the "Killing Fields". We had the opportunity to meet with (and have photos of) Mr. Chum Mey, one of the many victims and few survivors of the atrocities carried out by the Khmer Rouge. I purchased his book "Survivor" which tells in graphic detail of his experiences under the regime.

The tour of the area was a grim reminder of "Man's Inhumanity to Man", with cabinets full of the skulls of the unfortunate victims.

In 1979 Vietnam invaded and overthrew the dictatorship of the Khmer Rouge.

The Royal Palace, Phnom Penh

After lunch aboard ship we toured Cambodia's capital Phnom Penh. The Mekong River had now left us, going north to Laos, and we were on the Tonle River. Our trip included a visit to the Royal Palace and the Silver Pagoda, so named after the 5000 silver floor tiles there. Inside the Pagoda is a statue of Buddha crafted from pure gold, and dripping with over 2000 diamonds. Just north of the city centre is the Buddhist temple of Wat Phnom. Built in 1372, at 27 metres high it is the tallest religious building in the city. Getting around the city is best done by hiring a tuk-tuk, a sort of motorcycle with trailer attached, and very popular with tourists.

Next afternoon we set sail up the river towards Koh Chen, a village home to several workshops specialising in the manufacture of copper goods. Then back to the ship preparatory for a trip next morning to Oudong, from 1618 to 1866 the former royal capital of the country. Here we visited the newest and largest Buddhist monastery in the country, also serving as a study centre. Its interior is covered with paintings, both on the wall and on the ceiling......very impressive. The many children in evidence had just finished lunch, sitting cross-legged on the floor. We joined a blessing ceremony chanted by the monks, and then walked around the complex, where we encountered some other children selling curios. I bought a silver elephant as a memento of my visit to the temple. Then on by coach to Kampong Tralach, where a ride on an ox-cart had been arranged. This is the main form of transport in the countryside, carrying the harvest, hay, animals and even families. All I can say is they are welcome to it....I found it very uncomfortable and hard to keep my seat on it. The journey of around 25 minutes took us past rice fields and fisheries to the Tonje River where, thankfully, we rejoined our ship and sailed on to Kampong Chhnang, a busy port and market town in the wetlands. That evening we indulged in a Farewell Dinner, at which Cambodian girls and boys gave a demonstration of traditional dancing in traditional Cambodian costume.

After breakfast next day our cruise came to an end; we had been intended to sail on the lake to the city of Siem Reap but, being the dry season, the water level there was insufficient to accommodate our ship, so instead we travelled by coach through rural Cambodia to the country's faster-growing city. En route we called at Tai Phrom, once a flourishing Buddhist temple of some 12,000 monks but abandoned in the 13th century following an invasion by Siamese from the north. It was rediscovered in 1860 and rescued from the jungle's grip. Today it is notable for tree roots intertwining amongst the stonework, and for appearing in the film "Tomb Raider" with Angelina Jolie. Later we visited a school providing education for disadvantaged and orphan children (ODA). Here we were welcomed by a short talk from the school's director, and learned a little about its aims and methods. A full education is provided from kindergarten to university through dance, art, IT and English studies. We saw a short episode of such dances, and were then free to talk to the children and inspect their artwork, some of which was for sale. I purchased one of these, painted by an 11-year old girl, and it now hangs on my wall. Monies from these sales goes towards providing the children with free boarding at the school. Then we were on our way to the Shinta Mani Resort in the city, a top hotel. My room was on the ground floor, only yards away from its enticing swimming pool.

Next morning we took the coach to the Angkor Archaeological Park, with time to explore the Hindu temple of Angkor Wat. As many of us were 'Oldies' transport had been arranged for the Park's own police service to escort us right to the base of this magnificent ruin. Construction had begun in under King

Jayavarman in 790 A.D. and the complex became the capital of the Khymer Empire. However, by the end of the 12th century it had become a Buddhist temple and later was deserted, although never completely abandoned, which is why it is still in a good state of repair compared to other religious sites.

On our way out of the park I saw my first elephants, waiting by the roadside for tourists to clamber up and sit in the howdah. An impressive sight nonetheless. Back at the hotel I managed to join, with some others, in the swimming pool before going in for the Farewell Dinner that evening, which concluded with yet another display of dancing by Cambodian girls. They even managed to include me in their repertoire…. I think my flamboyant silk shirt had something to do with that!

Next morning it was, for me at least, up bright and early to take the mid-morning flight to Bangkok. I had fortunately made the acquaintance of an Australian doctor who had need of a wheelchair, and he managed to get me one also, together with the requisite badging. This came in very handy at both Bangkok and Heathrow airports where, without difficulty or delay, I was whisked through formalities. For the first time on this holiday I was glad of my "status", caused by breathlessness and the eventual discovery of fluid in my pleural cavity. I felt that I was lucky to have survived so long without problems, and my walking stick had been a godsend!

Arriving eventually at Heathrow I found that I would have to wait for over 4 hours for a seat on the next available coach, but when the earlier one arrived a very kind attendant found – having persuaded a lady to remove her excess baggage from the seat - that there was a space near the front. So, all was well that ended well, even having to take a taxi from Swansea bus station at 3.a.m. back to my apartment. It was a holiday of a lifetime (mine anyway) covering almost 500 miles by river, and which I am unlikely to repeat, but I will always have my memories and photos to aid in recalling it.

A Visit to Carew Castle and Tenby

With the Clydach Historical Society

2018

A somewhat chilly July morning saw thirty members foregather outside the Community Centre, to await the arrival of our J.T.Thomas coach, which was to take us first to Carew castle in Pembrokeshire, and later on to Tenby.

Carew Castle exterior, overlooking the Tidal Mill

This trip, arranged by our chairman Philip, duly departed at 9.a.m. and we were soon bowling down the M4 and on past Carmarthen. Arriving at the castle most of us sought the comfort of the newly-opened café, while we waited for the arrival of Mike our tour guide, one of several employed by the Pembrokeshire Park Authority. After a brief welcome he informed us that, due to the size of our contingent, we would only be getting the shortened version but, after more than an hour of walking and listening, we agreed that it had been just about right, and very interesting and entertaining. We were then free to further poke around, re-visit the café or walk down the lane to the Tidal Mill on the edge of the Carew river. The castle is situated on an area of flat land alongside the river some ten miles upstream from Pembroke, on top of what was once an Iron Age settlement.

Gatehouse of Carew Castle

Although still owned by the Carew family, now living in the Home Counties, the castle and grounds were in 1983 leased to the Park Authority for 99 years, and subsequent years have seen a lot of renovation and improvement. Further, because of its bat population living in one of the towers, and several species of rare plants, the castle has been designated an SSSI (site of special scientific interest). It is also home to a number of ghosts (we didn't meet any!). The first lady of the castle, who married its builder, was Princess Nest, who had some quite traumatic marriages after her husband's death, and who is known as the "White Lady". Another is the ghost of a Barbary Ape, who in the 17th Century was the companion of Sir Roland Rhys. When Sir Roland's son eloped with the daughter of a local merchant, said merchant went to him to protest, and the argument grew heated. The ape was set upon the merchant, who was lucky to escape with his life, and in doing so cursed Sir Roland. That night a terrible noise was heard and the servants, on entering his bedchamber, found bloodied Sir Roland lying dead alongside the ape, who was unmarked. Since then the ape has roamed the upper rooms, especially on stormy nights, making bloodcurdling noises.

Interior courtyard of Carew Castle

The castle suffered considerably during the English Civil War as Cromwell, not wishing to have a fortified neighbour on the doorstep of Pembroke Castle, blew up the kitchens and the outer wall. As a result, Carew Castle was soon abandoned and is today a romantic ruin.

Our onward visit to Tenby proved much more uneventful. We had four hours in the resort where most of us either had lunch, shopped, wandered the streets within the town walls, or simply sat and people-watched in the warm afternoon sunshine. Some hardy souls did descend to the beach but at around five-thirty we all boarded our luxury coach for the return journey, arriving at Clydach a little before seven p.m. Our thanks are extended to Philip for arranging this most informative and enjoyable day out, and we look forward the next one. Over to you, Philip.

Tenby Harbour

Llandudno

2019

Situated on the north coast of Wales, this is the jewel in the Welsh crown. Situated on the Creuddyn peninsula, it is the largest holiday resort in Wales. Nowadays the town owes so much to the Victorians, both in its buildings and in the town's layout, but its origins lie far back in the mists of time! In the 6th Century St. Tudno came and established a church on the Great Orme, the largest of the two headlands encompassing the sweep of the bay. That church was replaced in the 12th Century by another, built on the same site. We all know what Llan means (church) and Tudno devolved into Dudno. So said, the town took its name from the church and its founder.

The Great Orme, North face

However, St. Tudno was not the first inhabitant of the area. Over 4000 years ago prehistoric man was busy mining the Great Orme for its copper ore. Most of it is opencast, although there are also tunnels which present-day visitors can explore. Over the years the mines were abandoned and indeed covered up, and were only re-discovered in 1987. Today they rank alongside Stonehenge as a world-class tourist attraction. Spaced around the slopes of the Orme (207 metres high) are various prehistoric settlements, whilst its limestone is home to a varied selection of fauna and flora, and various sea-birds find homes on its sheer cliffs. Additionally, a herd of Kashmir goats roam the slopes, their ancestors having been presented to Queen Victoria as a gift.

Cafe-Restaurant at the top of the Great Orme

A little higher up the 'Orme' (its name derives from the Norse for sea-serpent – URM) can be found a restaurant and cafeteria (once home to the boxer Randolph Turpin), as well as an ex-lighthouse (now an hotel), and the termini of two of the means of access to the summit…the cable-car and the tramway. Both start from their bases on the North shore, near to the Halfre gardens at the foot of the Orme. Here in Happy Valley is a bandstand, and on Obscura Mound is a 'Camera Obscura' which gives a 360% view of the local area.

The start of Marine Drive

Around the base of the Orme runs Marine Drive, a 4-mile one-way toll road, whilst a little way along the promenade is the floral clock (which keeps accurate time), and the new lifeboat station. During the summer visitors can take the opportunity to travel around the town and out to neighbouring areas on a restored Routemaster London bus – well worth the modest charge.

A major attraction of the area is the pier, built in 1878, and at 700 metres is the longest in Wales. It is home to an amusement arcade, a café and bar and numerous kiosks, whilst at its sea-end is an area set aside for those wishing to try their hand at fishing. The landward end is dominated by the Grand Hotel, and from nearby runs the land-train which takes one along the promenade, past a multitude of hotels and guest-houses towards the quieter and sandier West shore.

Llandudno Pier

Here too, at Penmorfa was in the 1860's the home of Alice Liddle, the original Alice in Wonderland. Alice's father was Dean of Christ Church, Oxford, and had spent his honeymoon in the town. Later, his family took several holidays in the area before having a house (Pen Morfa) built near-to the beach. Dotted about the town along the town trail can be found various statues associated with the stories told to Alice by a family friend, Charles Dodgson, whose pen-name was Lewis Carroll

On a more personal note, I took an opportunity to travel by coach to Llandudno and stayed at the Risboro Hotel just off the sea-front. Here I met with the hotel's owners, the Chenery family, who are doing their best to upgrade the hotel fabric and décor. They gave a very warm welcome to me, and I found the food and evening entertainment - an excellent lady singer, and a drag artist, both family members - very good value. I also met with Minnie, one of their dogs. She is a small animal, but very prominent in a "soap" recently running on BBC1. 'Pitching Up' is a saga about the doings of a camp-site; this one is actually situated on Anglesey, and Minnie supposedly belongs to the site owner (played by Larry Lamb).

Minnie the dog

As for St. Tudno, he was reputedly the grandson of Seithyn, King of Dyfed in the 6th Century, whose son Seithenyn was blamed for letting the fertile lands of Gwaelod become inundated by the sea, so forming present-day Cardigan Bay. As a result, Tudno and his brothers left the area, moving to a monastery at Bangor-on-Dee. Later Tudno supposedly returned to dwell in a cave on the edge of the Great Orme, from where he preached Christianity to the stone-hutted occupants on the slopes of the Orme, before founding his church amongst them.

Llandudno street scene

Llandudno has today a well-laid-out town centre, with wide streets being ideal for shoppers and tourists to wander about without hindrance. Cafes and restaurants abound, and culture can be found at the North Wales Theatre and the International Art Gallery. Sundry buses will take you to the neighbouring towns of Rhyl, Conway, Bangor and even into the rugged interior of Snowdonia, whilst access by rail is via a branch line from Llandudno Junction. Two 3-day carnivals take place in the Mostyn Street area each year…the Victorian Festival in June, and in September the arts festival. The parish church nowadays is Holy Trinity, also in Mostyn Street, as too is the indoor shopping area of the Victoria Centre.

So there it is….Llandudno is a lovely town in a very special setting. But…if you DO feel like heading out somewhere, there are Edward 1st castles at Conway & Caernarvon, and smaller Welsh ones in the hinterland; gardens at Bodnant, a narrow-gauge railway at Llanberis, and a mini-railway at Bettws-y-Coed. And for the more adventurous there is, of course, Snowdon itself….either by rail from Llanberis or even walking/climbing to the café at the summit. You are not likely to become bored in this area; there is always something to do or somewhere to go if you only look for it. I enjoyed every minute of my stay in the town, and am looking forward to my next visit there.

The land-train at Llandudno

Cruising Around the Bay of Biscay

2019

This year, as a change from our annual pilgrimage to Scotland, I offered to take the largest part of my family on a cruise. Not any old cruise either, but on the **Britannia**, flagship of the P&O line. So, after a visit to our local travel agent, and the handing over of a large part of my available capital, I booked us on a week's cruise around the Bay of Biscay over the Easter holidays….had to be then as my three grandchildren were all still at school or college. None of the party had ever been on a cruise, and this one additionally provided them with the opportunity to land in France and Spain and try out their fledgling language skills.

Following several weeks of excitement, the day eventually arrived for us to begin our trip. Taxis dropped us off at our boarding point on the M4 to meet the coach taking us onward to Southampton, where we were to join the ship. From our home base in Swansea it was quite a long journey, but the children were buoyed up by anticipation and time passed quickly. All too soon we were at the docks, with our ship looming over us….all 140,000 tons of it, and our home for the next 7 days, together with over 3600 other passengers. Formalities at the port were quickly and efficiently dealt with, and we were soon aboard ship, and looking for our cabins. Luggage was being dealt with separately, and would eventually meet up with us. Our three girls (Imogen (17), Bryony (15) and Ceridwen (12) would be sharing a cabin near to my single one on the port side, whilst their parents had theirs starboard-side.

Imogen and Brian

Our evening meal was scheduled for 6 p.m., which was also the time for departing from Southampton. We were able to catch glimpses of the Isle of Wight as we passed, but then we were out in the open Channel, and heading for Cherbourg in northern France, where we were due to dock early next morning. Being such a large ship there was little or no sense of movement unless one looked over the side; inside the ship all was smooth and calm. After a mandatory life-jacket drill it was time for our evening meal, after which we were free to explore….which the girls did with abandon. The idea of "kids' clubs" was also jettisoned, and they sought instead to frequent the cafes, bars and shops on board. Somewhat foolishly (or generously, depending upon your point of view) I also said that any such purchases by the girls could be charged first to their on-board account and then onto **my** credit card). I'll know better next time….if there ever is one!

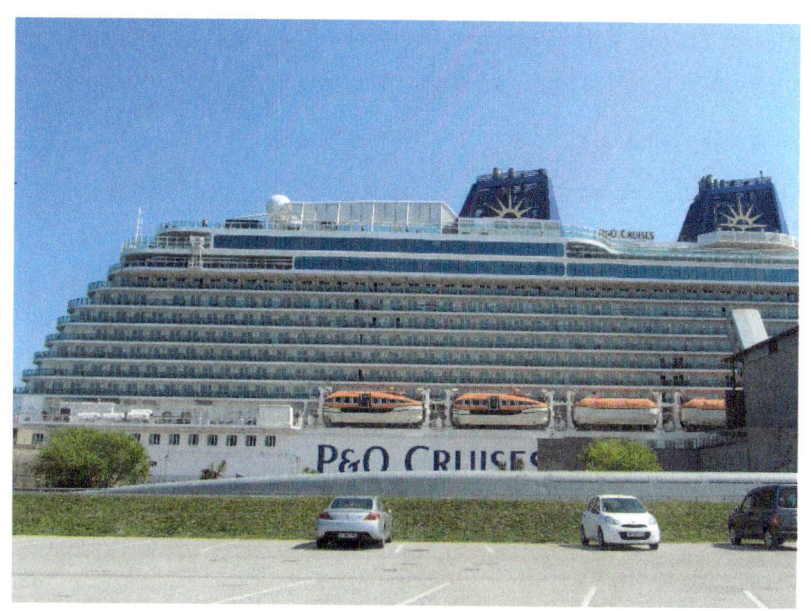

The Britannia

Next morning we found that we had already docked at Cherbourg. The day was pleasantly sunny, and after breakfast arrangements were made to walk into the town and see what was on offer. I had visited the town some years before, so the rest of the party set off without me. Instead, I contented myself with walking around the harbour and photographing what was there, as well as visiting the adjacent maritime museum. The others had a good walk around but, it being Easter Sunday, found that most shops were closed and their proposed shopping spree had to be postponed. Back at the ship it was time for more food, followed by the evening's entertainment which, as we were to find out, was top-class every evening. Each day games and quizzes were in evidence, as well as TV, films and music items. The following day was a "day at sea" as we travelled without incident down the length of the Bay, looking forward to the Captain's "Black Tie" Gala Reception (and the free drink!), before arriving early next morning at La Coruna on the north-west point of Spain, and known as the "Crystal City" due to the many glass-enclosed balconies of the tall apartment buildings facing the harbour.

The 3 girls: Bryony, Ceridwen and Imogen

Our weather had been of the "so far, so good" variety and next morning began in similar fashion. I had booked to go on the coach excursion to Santiago de Compostela, whilst the family once again spent time on board or around the port. I was looking forward to the journey as, many years ago now, my wife and I had travelled across northern Spain in our motorhome to arrive at this city on a pleasant and warm evening. However, the next morning turned wet and we had been unable to park near enough to the Cathedral of St. James to make the visit viable. So I had missed out then, and so determined that I would, on this occasion, make up for it.

Is it me, I wondered, or simply the workings of S*ds Law, but once again the weather had turned against me, and as we neared Santiago the rain began to descend. After a trip of just over an hour, we managed to walk to the Cathedral, which contains the mortal remains of St. James the Apostle, without getting too wet, but by then the light had deteriorated and good photography was out of the question.

The Mausoleum Santiago de Compostela, in which some of St James' bones are kept

Disappointingly, the building's impressive Baroque facade was festooned with scaffolding, as was - we soon discovered – also the interior, with builders' barriers diverting the crowd along unwanted routes. We did learn that 2020 was to be a Holy Year (when the Saint's Day falls on a Sunday, and 'indulgences' are granted to any visitor who makes it there on that day). I can only hope that the weather will be better for them than for me on the occasion of my visits. As a consequence, most of my time was spent in a nearby coffee shop…very welcome both for the coffee and the shelter it afforded. And a good book makes for a satisfying companion. Typically, by the time of returning arrived the rain had eased, and the journey back to the ship was incident-free .Here too they had had some rain, but now the sun was shining brightly upon the just and my family both!

Brian and Ceridwen

Life aboard went on much as anywhere would; despite there being so many persons on ship they were rarely evident in large numbers. Indeed, the most often we ever mingled with was at the evening entertainment, when the theatre was generally crowded. The shows proved very popular, and were extremely professional, backed by lighting and music of a high standard. The two nightly shows were flanked by early and later dinners, followed each evening by quizzes, or just drinkies in the various bars.

The pool of the Britannia

Our girls soon got into the swing of ship-board life, and the swimming pools proved most popular with them, as did the shops and the bars. The only potential downside were the tips, working out at £7 per person per day …including children…..and costs would have been sky-rocketing were it not for our travel agent, who had advised us that, by approaching the ship's Reception on the matter, we could indeed opt out of this charge. Significantly, P&O within a month had revised their policy and abandoned this means of rewarding the ship's staff, leaving it to the passengers to make their own decisions for future cruising.

One of my early concerns had been how the girls would react to on-board dining. We had been allocated to the *Oriental*

Restaurant, one of several similar about the ship, with an early dining slot.

Ceridwen and her father, Rob

To access this particular area we had to use two lifts, easy in principle but more difficult in practice as there was no direct passage between these, and the lifts were in any case in use by the multitude at that time of the evening. However, once at the location we were instructed to cleanse our hands and then proceed to the same table each night. The quality of the meals was very good, as were the choices on offer too, and we all coped well, with even the vegetarians amongst us managing to find acceptable menus. Despite there being an alternative "buffet" restaurant available throughout the day, we stuck to the principle of dining 'en famille' each evening, and on a couple of occasions even used our own restaurant for breakfast. There was also "High Tea" available mid-afternoon should we wish to take up the offer, but at other times throughout the day the 'Horizon' buffet provided good dining opportunities, with the added bonus of an excellent view over the sea.

At Bilbao

Our next port of call was Bilbao, set between two ranges of hills and either side of the river Nervion. It is the industrial and financial capital of the Basque country. The day had begun dry and warm, and our coach dropped us in the Old Quarter, with its fine architecture and enticing shops. Nearby was the piece de resistance, the Guggenheim Museum, a stone, titanium and glass masterpiece in its own right. We managed to by-pass the queues and infiltrate ourselves into the lower ground floor without payment, and looked around at the many objets d'art displayed there. To progress further would have cost some 9 euros each, amounting to a considerable sum for our party, so we withdrew and gazed instead at the bedecked sizable floral canine creation outside. Below us too was the Metro, with trams buzzing busily along its rails, and in the near distance could be seen the Bridge and Church of St. Anton. Once the girls were sated on ice creams we found a small supermarket, where their parents topped up their shopping bags with drink of various kinds. These were supposed to be declared on our return to the ship but in the event were not, and no-one questioned us as we carried them aboard.

The pool area on the upper deck

We had one more landfall to make, so overnight the ship made its way towards our Channel Island destination of Guernsey. However, en route we were advised that, due to an excessive sea swell, our tenders would not be able to load or disgorge passengers, and that the visit to that island was to be abandoned. It was a disappointing end to an otherwise interesting and exciting trip, and the ship slowly made its way up the English Channel towards Southampton, our port of disembarkation. However, the trip had served the family well; no one had been sea-sick, and all – the three girls in particular – had had a marvellous experience which will provide them with photographs and memories for many years to come.

Section C

Articles of Interest

Our Life In Motorhomes

Recent articles concerning owners' experiences of various motorhomes over the years prompted me to look up a few details concerning our own. We are not, you understand, of the breed that changes their 'mobile home' every few years, or in some instances months.

Back in 1978 we thought it might be a good idea to try motorhoming with our young children, then aged six and eight. My parents had just returned from living in Spain to settle near their grandchildren, so the chances for cheap Spanish holidays had vanished.

We hired a coachbuilt, and went to the north east for a week. Apart from the dishes shooting out of an overhead cupboard whilst cornering on Lindisfarne, the trip was a success so we tried again the following year.

This time to Cornwall, and, whilst not such a success, due to wet weather and misjudging the height of the vehicle, we felt that we might like to try a third year.

By this time, hire prices had escalated beyond our means, and a friend told us where there was a good opportunity to purchase a caravanette. We took the bait, visited the dealer, came to an arrangement, and, bingo, were now owners of our next holiday vehicle. The fact that it was smaller didn't deter the children, whilst I appreciated its lower roofline.

We had that 'van, a Bedford Buccaneer, for six years, during which we had the nearside rear window waterproofed (it let rain in like mad) and the whole vehicle resprayed.

The Bedford Buccaneer

We had only one serious mechanical flaw. After a service we were on our way to France when the camper broke down outside Wanstead tube station in London. The RAC were called, and the fault - a ripped wire in the distributor cap - was supposedly fixed. A few miles later on, in the Blackwall tunnel, we broke down again and had to be towed out by a police car. They were not amused, but when we told them that the RAC had just fixed us, the police called them out, and we were attended to just outside the tunnel. No further problem, luckily.

Our daughter slept above the cab, and our son in one of the stretcher beds in the Spacemaker lifting roof, whilst sundry clothes generally occupied the other. The main drawbacks with this type of roof consisted of having to be outside (in the rain, usually) to lift the roof, and a tendency to begin closing in high winds (our son was actually nicely folded up on one occasion with particularly high winds).

The Buccaneer with the top up

When it rained, the water permeated through onto the clothes or the sleeping bag of the occupant on that side. Visits to launderettes to use their dryer were not uncommon, and it was after one of these incidents near Weymouth that the kids eventually delivered their ultimatum: "get rid of it and buy a proper coachbuilt".

By 1986 we had clocked up around 125 nights and covered 29,000 miles in our Buccaneer. Not all this was mileage related to camping, of course, as the vehicle was used as both people-carrier and goods transporter. However, we had managed to visit Wales, Scotland, Yorkshire and Paris over the years, and had been very satisfied with its performance.

Now with rosier finances (and with an injection from my parents) we looked around for a replacement. This came from an unlikely source. By now my father had passed on and, whilst staying with mother for a weekend, she mentioned that one of her bridge partners was looking to part with her own Bedford coachbuilt, a long-wheelbase Advantura.

We all fell in love with it - who wouldn't after the restrictions of our own - and struck a deal, returning to collect it a couple of weeks later. The previous winter I had shown our children photographs of one of my own holidays with my parents in Andorra, and they were insistent that our first big trip was to that country.

After a couple of short outings, we prepared for the long trip to Andorra in the school summer holidays. By then we had discovered some of the vehicle's shortcomings.

There was no on-board toilet, so we had to use a Porta Potti in emergencies, as well as making full and proper use of site facilities. There was no wardrobe either, so a rail was fixed in the shower cubicle to accommoade coats and the longer shirts and dresses.

The Advantura

Unfortunately, it was impossible to stop water leaking out from the showerhead on the move, although the biggest casualty of this was some spare notes our son had secreted beneath the potti. The bank was not amused!

Additionally, to heat the water it was necessary to go outside to the gas heater at the rear of the vehicle and manually light it with a splint. Impossible in high winds, and unpleasant on dark, wet evenings. Still, we managed and, despite a puncture as we entered a campsite (the wheel changed next day via Europe Assistance) our three week trip through France and into the mountains of Andorra was deemed a success.

Family group outside the Advantura, 1986

It was not until August 1988 that we had our first of several problems. On a visit to southwest Scotland we parked outside Dundrennan Abbey. On our return, the motor just would not fire, so we called the RAC. The fault - alternator wiring - was fixed in a couple of minutes and we were off again. 1990 saw us marooned on a petrol station forecourt for an hour, waiting for the RAC to come and fix the same problem.

In 1991 the same fault occurred, this time in Crackington Haven, Cornwall. No mobile phones then, but there was a phone box in the car park. Again the RAC, and again an earth fault remedied in a matter of minutes. They were getting fed up with us, and in 1992 when the exhaust blew up on the A1 with an almighty bang, we received a warning that we should be looking to maintain the vehicle better. In fact, it was being looked after by a national transport chain, and only its age was against it.

The final straw came at Easter 1992, whilst at the Peterborough Show. The weather was foul (you may remember) and a three-year-old Swift Kontiki attracted our attention. The salesman came to inspect our Advantura with a view to part-exchange and found the 'van walls dripping wet.

Damp had become a major problem, and we held our breath whilst he went away and deliberated. However, he agreed to the deal, and we were soon to become proud owners of a smart and modern vehicle with, at last, a proper toilet compartment. The Advantura had served us well as a family holiday home for six-and-a-half years, but now, after 23,000 miles and almost 150 nights out, the time had come to move on.

It was not only the Advantura that had moved on; our children had decided that holidays with Mum and Dad no longer held the old appeal. So our Kon-Tiki was now used almost solely by us.

The Kontiki at the Viaduct de Garabit, France

The Kontiki caught in traffic outside Cologne

The next sixteen years saw us follow the Pilgrim route to Compostela, and head to France four times. We covered Eastern Germany, Ireland and Scotland and went on several club rallies as well as numerous awaydays.

In 1995 I was about to retire, so we sold our home and lived on a campsite for three months whilst I served out my notice. The motorhome served many different purposes, including a visit to my daughter in Essex to transport her, four kittens and many of her belongings to our new home in the Welsh borderlands.

I also lived in it on site for a week when my wife went into a hospital many miles from home. Over those sixteen years we covered 48,000 miles, spent almost 500 nights away, and visited a good few hundred different campsites.

It wasn't all roses; one day we discovered that the overcab bed was sodden, and that the whole of the front roof area had been letting in water. This model was apparently prone to this, and our supply dealer worked hard to dry out the area and reseal the body.

At times major works were required to both body and the mechanics; a tree branch pierced the outer skin in a French orchard, a new clutch was called for just before we were due to replace one which took flight one evening across the A1, I sideswiped a tree with the front bumper on another French holiday, and a water pump had to be replaced as were on our way to join an overseas trip.

Eventually, damp raised its ugly head again, and the whole of the roof and one side had to be replaced. I had, by now, had enough and although we had got good use from our "Connie", visiting many places and making many friends through the Swift Owners Club, we were thinking about her replacement. When we did at last upgrade to a modern, and more comfortable motorhome, we were in some ways sorry to see her go.

So, in 2007, we went to the motorhome show at the NEC in Birmingham. There were vehicles of all types, sizes and prices, but could we find one to suit us?

We called in at a dealer near to home a few weeks later. Again, hundreds of 'vans to choose from, but the only one that appealed to us was a new Bürstner, and already sold. Could we order one?

"No problem" was the reply, but in the end there was, and a delivery time for the correct vehicle was way in the distance. Eventually, a friend told us of a Bürstner dealer far away, but in May 2008 we took delivery from them of the Ford-based Nexxo t660.

Before we collected the motorhome, we had it "paintsealed", a step we have not regretted. We also ordered a Silver Screen, had the oven relocated to beneath the hob, and a microwave installed in its place.

For the first time we had cruise control, power steering, reversing camera, garage storage, a full-size fridge, a fixed bed, concealed safe, insect screens and swivelling captain chairs. You'll notice the lack of a TV! We have never taken one with us, and never, ever, missed it.

The Nexxo in France, enroute to Italy in 2008

A quick trip down the M5 to Van Bitz saw us equipped with their Strikeback and Batter Matter systems, and within the month we were ready for our first adventure in our new home. So, to France and on through into Italy.

The motorways in the North were amazing through the mountains, either crossing high bridges, or diving in and out of tunnels. Our Ford Transit performed admirably giving us a trouble-free run down to Pisa.

Here we suffered a setback. Despite the alarm, we were broken into via the habitation door, and only by good fortune returned in time to scare off the intruders. On our return home, we fitted a security cover over it, provided by Brightlock, and trusted that any further attempt to gain unauthorised entry would be thwarted.

Two of the grandchildren in the Nexxo

To date our Nexxo has covered 7740 miles and we have spent 76 nights out in her. We now look forward to many more days of travel and nights spent in the comfort of our home on wheels, whilst meeting many more people of all types and in several countries, and seeing places which, without our motorhome, we would not be able to travel to.

Maureen in the Nexxo

Hidden Treasure – Hales View Farm

Two miles outside Cheadle, Staffs, on the B5417 Oakamoor road, our eyes were opened wide as one of England's follies - Hales View Farm - suddenly came into view. "We must have a look at this." we enthused. THIS being a complex of huge brick barn-like structures with ornate decoration and pictorials built into them. Coincidentally, the camp site we were looking for - Hales Hall - lies immediately opposite so we were able to book in first, and then explore Hales View Farm at our leisure.

And leisure is what is needed if you are to do this amazing place justice. As we walked around the outside, examining the fountains, the statuary, cuppolas, old stonework - relics of a former age and former glories - we came face to face with the man himself. Les Oakes, twinkly-eyed, mid fifties and a shrewd businessman, was born on the adjacent Lower Grange Farm. Over 20 years ago he decided to erect buildings to house a collection of memorabilia second to none. To date there are three of these buildings on site and a fourth is well under construction, though Les is currently in dispute with Staffordshire Moorlands Council over planning permission for this block. As the buildings are on agricultural land and intended for agricultural use, i.e. storage, Les feels that no such permission was required. And, as he says himself, he is not too good on paper so does not really know what the place is intended to look like: he makes it up as he goes along with whatever material he has to hand.

Incorporated into the brickwork are foundation stones and stone tablets from public buildings, a Wesleyan chapel and a public bath, windows from stately homes, and even a complete frontage from the Trumpet public house, Hanley. Designs in a lighter brick of horses and waggons show up well from a distance, and a clock high up on the gable declares the time in bold Roman numerals.

One of the buildings housing the collections

Once inside, the older generation of visitors will quickly recognise items from their own historical period. One building is crammed with an incredible collection of vehicles, ranging from a World War 1 ambulance to a Francis Burnet motorcycle, a black horse-drawn hearse to an early 20th century red fire engine. Other buildings house a variety of farm implements, horse-drawn carriages, gipsy caravans, motor vehicles and prams, cycles and even a World War 1 field kitchen. An upstairs museum houses a fantastic collection of memorabilia - radios, toys, bottles, a complete PABX switchboard, and household implements - you want it, you will find it here. Bring the grandparents for a touch of nostalgia, and the children for a living insight into times now well past. Just imagine milk delivered from a pony and trap at 2d per pint - or trying to mangle the weekly wash.

We eventually departed several hours later, wishing Les every success in his endeavours to finish the building of yet another of his creations. Hale View Farm is certainly well worth a visit, both to see items of yesteryear which might otherwise have been lost, and to marvel at the all-embracing persistence of a man who has accumulated an impressive and sizeable collection, and erected a unique assembly of buildings in which to house them. Almost as a sideline, Les also operates a thriving business in conventional building materials, both new and reclaimed, and can be relied upon to produce anything from old paving and tiles to new window frames and sanitary-ware. If you are willing to do a deal, you will find Les is too. We left him thriving on it.

The reclamation business thrives as well

Oh yes, back to the campsite across the road. Hales Hall was once aminor stately stately home, now somewhat in disrepair but at least still in use as the site's focal point. There is a children's games room, a bar and a restaurant (which incidentally does a good-value three-course Sunday roast). Behind the Hall is a large heated swimming pool open in season to campers, and further behind yet is a small shop. The site facilities are modern and well-equipped, lacking only at present a dish-washing area. There is ample camping space in the park, which includes areas for rallies and holiday homes.

View from the Campsite at Hales Hall

For the children the site has a small play-area, and - at the far end - an interesting pets' corner. Oh, and if you tire of walking, you might be lucky enough to encounter the tractor-pulled cart giving rides to the children. All in all, a pleasing site and a most fascinating visit.

Development of the Westgate Chronicle

"Accept my hallowed labour now,

I do it unto Thee"   (Charles Wesley)

My spell as Editor of the Westgate Chronicle covered the years 1991-1995, although I had sat on the Committee for some while previous to that. From its inception the group had been known as the Publicity Committee, concentrating on "News of the Church Family". Issue No.1 in July 1978 publicised the activities both of our church and those of others in the circuit, as well as the Junior Church's impending visit to Wicksteed Park. Our minister Douglas Tunbridge exhorted members (the start of the Minister's Letter) to read/write/care about each other through the "Personal Column". The monthly church calendar was also set out, later joined by the Rotas, and listing applicable church personnel.

Westgate Church, Peterborough

Of course, it could not succeed on such a narrow base alone, so gradually news of church events was added to by articles, stories and poems from members, and news of such as the Church Meeting, the URC & Methodist Assembly/Conference and material lifted from the Methodist Recorder. This kind of "journalism" set the magazine's tone for many years. Jokes (and sometimes cartoons) also made an appearance, as well as more serious items such as Birthdays, the Cradle Roll, and reports from groups such as the Friendship Circle, the Jasper Club, and the Boys and Girls' Brigades. Competitions and quizzes crept in, and Sue King introduced a Children's Page. Gradually articles were being submitted by both adult and junior members, as well as culled from external sources, and over time the magazine became both accepted and expected.

However, production was time-consuming and, to a degree, costly, and a contribution of 10 pence per copy was asked for. Initially material was typed by Pam Mager, later by Olive Gardner. To this was added "cut & paste", and in the late eighties the magazine's cover was produced in colour. Now it is back to black & white on coloured paper. It has, however, almost always featured a reproduction of our church, even during the dark days following the serious fire in 1983 when we had to walk to Mayor's Walk for services. Over the years, production methods improved greatly, moving from typing to typesetting and from duplicating to photocopying to printing. The next two improvements were photographs in monochrome, then in colour, and the upgrading of the paper in use. The quality of the magazine nowadays is a thousand times better than that of the first issue, an improvement of which the current editorial team must be very proud. It should however be remembered that they have access to technology that was not in existence in the early days, and throughout its life the editorial teams have all striven to produce the best that was possible, given the circumstances.

Making the news

THE city's Westgate Church is celebrating the 200th edition of its parish magazine.

The church, situated in the city centre, launched the Westgate Chronicle in 1978.

During the years, the monthly magazine has recorded many changes in the church, including several ministers, and featured numerous members of the congregation.

The church fire in May 1983, and the building of the present Westgate Centre, were among major issues reported by the voluntary magazine committee.

Another change is now imminent with the current editor of the Chronicle, Brian Davies handing over the reins to another church member, Joanne Vernon, **pictured above**.

Mr Davies, who has been editor for five years, and involved with the magazine for eight, is planning to move away from Peterborough. For the time being, he will look after the church's bookstall.

(Photo: 9501785/14)

Handing over the reins

I have been asked to recall anything pertaining to the production of the magazine in my day. I recall members of the team in the vestry trying to coax a recalcitrant duplicating machine to do its best, and then sorting the pages across the tables before stapling. At times copy was late in coming, causing a production delay. Much time was expended by members of the editorial team in their efforts to produce the Chronicle. Later, photocopying of the covers in colour was carried out (by me) at the Thomas Cook head office. Later we used the services of Kall-Kwik in the city centre, and then a printing company in Werrington. Next, production was taken over by the Vernons, using their resources, and today....well, *you* tell *me*! But this I *can* say, it has been both an honour and a pleasure to have served the church community in this way, and following my retirement, on moving away, in 1995 to the Welsh borders, it initially left a large gap. Now, that has been replaced by my taking up the position of organist in my local Methodist chapel, and that gap has been filled, but I will not forget my time at Westgate.

Sawney Bean
Eating One's Cake and Having It....

"The story of Sawney Bean"

Are you feeling hungry? For fame, or attention? Or simply for….. FOOD?

Back in the 1500's, a baby boy was born in East Lothian, Scotland. His father was a hedge trimmer and ditch digger, and the little boy, now known as "Bean", was expected to take his place in the family trade. However, he soon realised he had little appetite for such hard work and eventually, taking up with a vicious woman, they transferred to the coastal area south of Girvan. Living in a cave some 25 yards deep, and blocked at high tide by deep water, they produced a family of some 8 sons, six daughters, eighteen grandsons and fourteen granddaughters, mostly by way of incest.

So, one might wonder, how did the group (or clan) provide food for all these dependents? Well, lacking an inclination for regular work, they devoted time to laying ambushes at night so as to rob and murder individuals or small groups of travellers. The main road, which nowadays climbs up a steepish cliffside to its summit before descending again to the level, at that time lay alongside the beach, and the bodies of those unfortunates who could not escape the clutches of the clan were brought back to the cave, where they were dismembered…..and eaten. Left-overs were pickled for future use.

Entrance to the cave

Yes, these bodies were the staple food of the cave's inhabitants, whilst discarded body parts would at times wash up on nearby beaches. These, together with the disappearances of many people, did not go unnoticed by local villagers but, as the clan stayed in the caves by day and did their grisly work at night, the villagers were unaware of the murderers living nearby. However, following further disappearances, several searches were organised to find the culprits. One such actually took notice of the large cave but could not believe that anything human could be living in it. In a frustrated quest for answers, several innocent persons were lynched, whilst suspicion often fell on local innkeepers, as they would have been the last to see many of the missing people alive.

Eventually, what went around came around (as per the saying!). A married couple riding back from a fair on one horse was ambushed but the man, being skilled in combat, managed to hold off the clan with sword and pistol. They mauled the wife when she fell to the ground, but at the appearance of a large group of fairgoers the Beans fled. News of this atrocity reached the ears of King James VI of Scotland and a large manhunt with a team of 400 men and several bloodhounds discovered the previously overlooked cave in Bennane Head. The interior was littered with human remains, having been the scene of many murders and cannibalistic acts. The clan was captured alive and taken in chains to the Tolbooth Gaol in Edinburgh, and thence to either Leith or Glasgow for execution without trial. Males were castrated, had their hands and feet cut off, and allowed to bleed to death. The women and children, after watching their menfolk die, were burned alive.

Site of the beachside road

Two anecdotes relating to this and other cannibalistic acts....

It is said that one of Bean's daughters had previously left the clan's cave and settled in Girvan, where she planted a Dule Tree (*). This became known as the "Hairy Tree". After the family's capture, the daughter's identity became known to angry locals, who hanged her from a bough of the Hairy Tree.

Around the same period, a certain thief living in a den with his wife and children, and existing for many years by killing and eating young people, were captured and burned alive, save for a one-year-old girl who was saved and brought up in Dundee. At the age of 12 years she was found guilty of similar acts, and condemned to be burned alive. When a multitude of people followed her to execution she turned to them and with cruel taunts shouted…"Why do you rail at me as if I had done such a terrible act, contrary to the nature of Man? I tell you that if you did but know how pleasant the taste of man's flesh was, none of you would avoid eating it".

(*) Dule Tree…probably a tree whose use was designated by local chiefs as a "Hanging" tree.

Sawney Bean

Sawney Bean at the Entrance of His Cave. Note the woman in the background carrying a severed leg.

Born	Alexander Bean East Lothian, Scotland
Other names	Sawney
Children	14.

Sawney Bean is often regarded as mythical figure, but what is certain is that the practice of cannibalism was rife in the western areas of Scotland, especially Galloway, which was also well-known for its many robber hideaways. Dates may also have been adjusted by much story-telling.

The Mumbles Railway, Swansea

Or

"The World's First Passenger Railway"

Much of the world seems to have heard of Blackpool, on the north-west coast of Lancashire, and its golden sands, the Tower ballroom, its lights in November, and of course its famous tramway. But have you come across that other famous railway, at the other end of the country? Today, Swansea is Wales's second city, a bustling metropolis which has recovered well from the aerial pounding it took in 1941 from German bombers. But, prior to that period, Swansea was an industrial seaport of note, with ironworks, copperworks, limestone quarries and coalmines all linked by road, rail, river and canal, and flanked by some of the most beautiful scenery in the country.

A few miles to the west of Swansea, along a flat but scenic coast road, lies the village of Oystermouth, with its Norman castle, and adjacent to it is the Mumbles. The name is probably a mispronunciation of the French "les Mamelles", meaning female breasts, which the rocks do indeed mimic. The area houses a collection of buildings squeezed together before the winding coastal road out has to ascend a steep hill. Nowadays the area's main attractions are the pier, with its lifeboat shelter and the nearby lighthouse, and the wonderful view across Swansea bay. But back in the early 19th Century a big problem was how to move the limestone which was quarried out from the surrounding rocks, and which was in great demand by the industrial areas around Swansea. There was at that time no coastal road facilitating "supply and demand", and it was not until 1804 that an Act of Parliament allowed a "Company of Proprietors" to form and to lay down rails for the operating of horse-drawn wagons needed to carry quarried limestone from kilns on the Gower and coal from the Clyne Valley to wharves at the embryonic port of Swansea. So the Oystermouth Railway Company came into being.

In 1807, approval was given to the carrying of passengers along this route, and "tourists" flocked to see and make use of this novel form of travel. Dating from 25th March of that year, and using refurbished mineral wagons, it became the first railway in the world to carry passengers. However, towards the end of the 1820's a turnpike road was constructed between Swansea and Mumbles. Running parallel to the railway, it deprived it of much of its traffic, and in 1826 a decision was taken to stop carrying passengers. But in 1855 the then owner decided to upgrade the railway, and re-introduced the horse-drawn passenger service. Horses continued to be used until 1877, when they were largely replaced by steam locomotives, although a dispute between the line's operator and the locomotive owner (sound familiar?) delayed full introduction of the latter until 1896. In 1893 the railway was extended from Oystermouth to Southend, and in 1898 on to the Mumbles pierhead. 1900 saw Swansea become the first Welsh town to have electric tramcars on its streets, but the steam-powered Mumbles Railway had to wait until after the First World War for its next great improvement. In 1927 the slower steam trains were phased out and 1929 saw electrification using overhead cabling, which meant that larger and more comfortable "tramcars" could be utilised. A fleet of 11, later extended to 13, was brought into use. Each car could hold 106 passengers, and capacity per run was increased by coupling two cars together, giving rise to the terminology "train". Between Swansea's Rutland Street terminus to Mumbles Pier, a total of 12 stations had been constructed, and on busy summer days these and the trains would have been in full operation.

Mumbles Pier

The 1950s saw the start of a revolution in the country's road transport as bus travel became the 'norm', spreading more widely and with lower costs than had rail. This was contributed to by the Beeching Plan which truncated or eliminated a great number of the country's rail lines, and the Mumbles Railway was no exception. In 1958 the line was bought by the South Wales Transport Company which ran Swansea's buses and coaches, and their intentions were soon made clear. The first stage of the line's closure was the stretch between Southend and the Pier, which was converted to roadway to allow buses access to the pierhead. But finally, on January 5th 1960, the last train ran into Swansea to the accompaniment of huge crowds, both on and off the cars. The remainder of the railway was then closed down, track and equipment dismantled and the cars broken up for scrap. All that remains (or did) of this enterprise is a car cab outside the National Waterfront Museum at Swansea Marina and a tramcar sold to the Middleton Railway in Leeds and subsequently destroyed by arson. Many people then, as today, felt the railway's closure to be a short-sighted cost-saving move, but the tourist industry had not at that time gathered apace. Today, what would the city give to have such an attraction running along the great curve of the Bay, bringing visitors from all over the world, a veritable "Blackpool in the South"? Or possibly, even better!

Acknowledgements to Wikipedia, and to "Rocking Rolling Riding", a pictorial memento of the Mumbles Railway by David Benyon. Copyright held by Bryngold Books. Some photos by Brian G Davies

Brian G Davies

Brian G Davies lives in Swansea and is the author of the poetry anthology A Fountain Stirred as well as numerous travelogue articles that have been published in the magazines Innovate and The Wolfian over the last few years. These include reports on holidays across Italy, to Turkey, North Wales, and to Devon.

About the Author

Born in 1933 in South London of Welsh parentage, Brian was at the start of World War Two one of London's evacuees. Having spent a year as such in a small South Wales mining village he was then sent as a boarder to King's School, Ely in Cambridgeshire, where he remained until the war's end. Returning home in 1945, Brian transferred to Alleyn's College, Dulwich, and in 1952 was called up for National Service, initially at the Tower of London then posted to the Buffs (Royal East Kent Regiment) in Canterbury, before eventually joining the R.A.E.C. Most of this period was served as an educational Sergeant Instructor in Singapore.

Following his demob, Brian spent three years studying to qualify as a teacher. After some years as such in various schools he withdrew from the teaching profession and turned instead to commerce as a management consultant, working for various "blue-chip" companies. During this period he met Maureen, his wife-to-be, also a teacher, and they had two children. Over a considerable period they owned several motorhomes and spent many holidays travelling throughout the U.K. and on the continent. This enabled them to indulge their passion for exploration and travel while broadening the experiences of their children. Amongst their travels they followed the Pilgrim Route to Compostela, visited Singapore, crossed the Canadian Rockies by motorhome, cruised up the Inside Passage to Alaska, and ascended several of France's highest passes.

His poetry book "A Fountain Stirred" can be bought at **https://www.amazon.com/Fountain-Stirred-Brian-G-Davies/dp/1500683426/**

Printed in Great Britain
by Amazon